NATURE IN MUSIC

AND OTHER STUDIES IN
THE TONE-POETRY
OF TODAY

NATURE IN MUSIC

AND OTHER STUDIES IN
THE TONE-POETRY
OF TODAY

BY

LAWRENCE GILMAN

Essay Index Reprint Series

BOOKS FOR LIBRARIES PRESS, INC.

FREEPORT, NEW YORK

146182

First published 1914
Reprinted 1966

Some

"And shall not Loveliness be loved forever?"
—Euripides.

CONTENTS

I

NATURE IN MUSIC

NATURE IN MUSIC

"Nature consists not only in itself objectively, but at least just as much in its subjective reflection from the person, spirit, age, looking at it, in the midst of it, and absorbing it: faithfully sends back the characteristic beliefs of the time or individual . . . falls like a flat elastic veil on a face or like the moulding plaster on a statue."—*Walt Whitman*.

TONAL LANDSCAPES

"How long will you let the houses press you down? How long will you shut yourself up in the prison of smoky cities?" cried St. Jerome to the monk Heliodorus, while praising the beauty of God's solitudes. In this exhortation the excellent hermit was illustrating, some fifteen centuries in advance, the theory of an ingenious philosopher of our own day, M. Pierre Janet, who holds that those who, at different times in the history of the world's civilization, have manifested a strong attraction toward the natural world, have always been persons of a definite and particular type: emotional, subject to exaltation of mood, impatient of hampering traditions, essentially anti-conventional. Mr. Havelock Ellis, in his study of the psychology of the love of wild Nature, characterises all such persons as, in a greater or less degree, "temperamentally exceptional." In the strongest and simplest manifestations of the type, these lovers of wild Nature have been persons who were instinctively repelled by their ordinary environment; "the real world of their average fellow-men seemed to them unreal, and they were conscious of a painful sense of inadequacy toward it; they sought new and stronger stimulants, a new Heaven and a new earth."

This modern view of the cause and his-

tory of the love of Nature thus affords a
comfortable meeting-ground for two op-
posing philosophic camps: for those who,
on the one hand, have held the tradi-
tional view that an imaginative suscepti-
bility to Nature originated with Rousseau and the nineteenth-century Romantics, and those who hold that, on the con-
trary, the natural world has always, in
all ages, had its allure for the human
imagination. Thus Chateaubriand, who
had small use for mountains except as
"the sources of rivers, a barrier against
the horrors of war," is balanced by
Petrarch, who, climbing Mont Ventoux,
in Provence, in 1335, observed that his
soul "rose to lofty contemplations" on
the summit. Goldsmith objected that in
Scotland "hills and rocks intercept every
prospect"; yet Milton had savoured with
extraordinary vividness the beauty and
the awe of external nature—what magic
there is in his

NATURE IN MUSIC

" . . . Sabean odours from the spicy shore
Of Araby the blest."

We are thus invited to agree that at all times—though only in the case of a few uncommon persons—the fascination of the natural world has laid its hold upon a certain type of mind and spirit; and that Rousseau and the Romantics, although they were not discoverers of a new wonder-realm, yet opened wide its gates to their own and to succeeding generations. We are to find in Jerome, and in St. Augustine when he is rejoicing in "the manifold and various loveliness of sky and sea and earth," confessors of the same passion for the picturesque that, centuries later, swayed such visionary rebels as Rousseau and Wordsworth, Byron and Shelley, Keats and Whitman; and we perceive that when the punctilious and gentle Addison declared, in 1705, that the Alps as seen from the Lake of Geneva formed "one of the most ir-

regular misshapen scenes in the world,"
he was merely anticipating, for example,
Sir Leslie Stephen, who, two hundred
years later, could say of wild scenery that
it "derives half its charm from the occult
sense of the human life and social forms
moulded upon it," and who shrank from
the Alps as being "unbearably stern,"
tolerable only by virtue of "the picturesque society preserved among its folds."
For neither the world nor the heart of
man alters greatly during the years,
though we look from within outward
through eternally different eyes.

The strongest appeal of natural beauty
has always, then, been chiefly to indi-
viduals of emotional habit, and especially
to those of untrammelled imagination and
non-conformist tendencies: in other
words, to poetically minded radicals in
all times and regions. It is probable that
the curious and enlightened inquirer,
bearing in mind these facts, would not be
surprised to find, in studying the various

expressions of this attraction as they are recorded in the arts, that the uniquely sensitive and eloquent art of music has long been the handmaid of the Nature-lover; and he would be prepared to find the Nature-lover himself appearing often in the guise of that inherently emotional and often heterodox being, the music-maker.

This is, indeed, the case. The history of creative music is rich in attempted transcriptions of what Henry More called "the Outworld." There have been landscapists in music ever since Don Marco Ucellini, court conductor to the Duke of Modena, composed in 1669 his "Sinfonie Boscareccie," or "Wood Symphonies." Even before him, the Englishman John Mundy was writing pieces for the virginal which constituted a vague and tentative order of descriptive nature-painting—as, for example, a "Fantasia" wherein he assumes to portray "A Clear Day," "Lightning," "Thunder," "Calm

Weather." Indeed, a large part of the early history of instrumental programme-music is concerned with chronicling more or less determined attempts at landscape-painting on the part of various composers enamoured of picturesque titles. The student delving in the music of the seventeenth and eighteenth centuries will find a long succession of "Forest" symphonies, "Spring" symphonies, and pastoral pieces of a varying degree of naïveté: as certain harpsichord pieces of the Frenchman Couperin,—"Les Pavots," "Le Verger Fleuri," "Les Guirlands," "Le Reveille Matin," "Le Point du Jour," "Les Bergeries," "Les Abeilles"; or the famous "L'Allegro, Il Penseroso, ed Il Moderato" of Handel, with its attempted denotement of running streams, winds, bird songs; or the singularly elaborate tonal portraiture of the Venetian, Antonio Vivaldi (1680-1743), who, in his "The Four Seasons," discourses with remarkable and explicit detail of such matters

as Spring and its "flowering meadows"
and "rustling leaves," the heat and lan-
guor of Summer, the hunts and harvest
festivals of Autumn, the rigors, "terrible
wind," ice and cold of Winter; or the
"Portrait musical de la Nature" of Jus-
tin Heinrich Knecht, which anticipated
Beethoven's Pastoral Symphony by a
quarter of a century; and he will of
course note the naïve pictorialism of
Johann Sebastian Bach, and the equally
ingenuous Nature-painting to be found
in the oratorios of the estimable Josef
Haydn.

Perhaps it will not be amiss at this
juncture to recall what has been formu-
lated by the æstheticians as to the methods of the composer who essays in his
music a suggestion of external things—a
landscape or a seascape, a sunset or a
wind over the sea, or the odours of night
in the fields.

An English theorist, Mr. William
Wallace, has concisely defined and char-

acterised this kind of tone-painting by describing it as that order of music "which attempts to excite a mental image by means of an auditory impression." The writer of delineative or suggestive music—"programme music," as it is unsatisfactorily but conveniently designated —proceeds somewhat, as we know, after this fashion: By associating with his music a title, motto, or descriptive passage, he establishes a receptive condition in the mind of the hearer; his task is then to address the imagination of this auditor by the use of certain analogies, certain musical symbols, which will express and fulfil the concept which the title or superscription of the piece has evoked.

We have spoken of "musical symbols." There are two fundamentally different types of musical idea. On the one hand, we have the kind of musical idea which has no other reason for being than to embody an idea of beautiful utterance in the mind of the composer. On the other hand, we have the type of idea which is deliberately conceived and fashioned to excite, in Mr. Wallace's phrase, "a mental image"—either by direct tonal imitation, as of bird-notes, thunder, the shriek and whistle of wind; or more subtly, as in the suggestion of flowing water, dawn, moonlight, cloud forms, by imaginative analogies of colour and design; or, yet more subtly and reconditely, to communicate a particular mood, a definite state of feeling. It is of course true that if an idea of this latter type issues from the creative imagination of a genius, it will be valuable and potent *as music* in addition to its fitness and success as an expressional agent; but it will be so only, as it were, accidentally. For an example of the first type of idea, one might instance the opening measures of the Andante of Beethoven's Fifth Symphony, or the famous oboe melody in the slow movement of Schubert's Symphony in C-major, or any page from the chamber-music

20

of the classicists. Examples of the second type—ideas having an extra-musical intention—are nowhere more perfect and abundant than in the works of that supreme master of tonal portrait-ure, Richard Wagner; for the "leading-motives" of the Wagner music-dramas range through the entire gamut of tonal expression, from delineation of externals —the winds, waters, landscapes of the earth, and the outward aspects and con-cerns of man—to an exposition of the se-cret processes of the human heart and the loftiest aspirations of the spirit.

But let us contrast two specific exam-ples of both methods: the method of the "absolute" musician, and the method of the writer of music that seeks to delin-eate or suggest. For the first, consider that perfect flower of the genius of Jo-hannes Brahms, the lovely and meditative Intermezzo in E-major from the set of piano pieces known as Opus 116 (No. 2). Here is a perfect example of "absolute" music—self-contained, wholly single in intention, having no other aim or function than to discharge the mind of the composer of its burden of inspiration. Now contrast with this the nobly poetic piano piece, "In Deep Woods," of Edward MacDowell, from the group of tone-poems which he calls "New England Idyls." Here, too, is music of lovely and meditative beauty; but, unlike the Brahms piece, it is not single in intention. To begin with, it bears a title deliberately intended to engage the imagination of the hearer; and it has also this superscription, designed to enforce and particularise the significance of the music:

> "Above, long slender shafts of opal flame;
> Below, the dim cathedral aisles:
> The silent mystery of immortal things
> Broods o'er the woods at eve."

It is evident at the start that here is music with a purpose beyond that of making an effect of sheer musical beauty. That purpose is to effect, by means of suggestive analogies of character — breadth and solemnity of movement, mysterious majesty in harmonic colouring and melodic design—an enrichment and intensification of the images aroused in the mind of the hearer by the title and superscription of the piece. In brief, it aims to paint a picture and provoke an associated mood. Thus it has at once a more complex intention and a more complex effect than has the typical piece of Brahms. The material with which Brahms dealt in his Intermezzo was exclusively musical material; whereas MacDowell in his vivid little tone-poem exerts not only that inarticulate eloquence which belongs peculiarly to music, but also the concrete, precise, and definite eloquence of the poet, and the pictorial function of the painter. Indeed, the detractors of this very modern but also very ancient kind of music deprecate it upon precisely that ground: that it is not "self-contained"; that it needs the aid of words—a text, a motto, title, superscription—in order that it may accomplish its object and speak definitely to the imagination. The answer is, of course, that this order of music is a complex form, like the opera, the oratorio, and the song, none of which is independent of a text or commentary of some sort. The programmatic piano piece or symphony is precisely as "self-contained" and as "pure" as is the song or the music-drama. Each is dependent for its full realisation upon an element external to itself: the song, upon words in the mouth of the singer; the opera, upon words sung, action represented, or, very often, upon so flagrantly external a thing as the display and movement of scenery. The writer of descriptive piano music or orchestral pieces merely presents his defining element—his text—in the form of a published title, superscription, or "argument," and then proceeds to enlarge upon it. In the song, the opera, the oratorio, the definition of the music synchronises with its actual performance; in the tone-poem for orchestra or piano, the definition is stated in advance. The music written by Wagner to depict the magic flames of Loge bears the same necessitous and organic relationship to the coloured steam of the stage mechanic as the music of Debussy's "Après-midi d'un Faune" bears to the poem of Mallarmé which he indicates in the title of that famous and exquisite orchestral idyl.

The musical landscapist is, as we have seen, a very familiar apparition in musical history; but he has not always been an impressive figure there. His early attempts at nature-painting were for the most part crude, childish, and inept—either imitation of the baldest and feeblest kind, or mere musical sentimentalising, barren of artistic dignity or visualising imagination. There were giants in those days, but they were excellent and memorable in other fields than that of tonal landscape-painting. It is true that there were exceptions. In the nature-music of Couperin, Rameau, Gluck, and Bach, for example, there are admirable passages of descriptive writing. Later, in the hands of the resourceful and ingenious Haydn, the art of naturalistic depiction assumed a more important aspect. In "The Creation" and "The Seasons" there is nature-painting which is often remarkable for its genuine power and felicity. Haydn was, indeed, considerably more noteworthy as a writer of programme-music than as a composer of gracefully superficial symphonies, sonatas, and string quartettes, despite the importance of his contribution to the history of musical form. Still later we find the Romantic composers of the early nineteenth century essaying, with various degrees of impressiveness, tonal portraiture inspired by what the poet of "The Excursion" piously called "God's works in His visible creation"—as (for random instances) Beethoven in his "Pastoral" symphony; Berlioz in his 'Fantastic" and "Harold in Italy" symphonies; Spohr in his "Consecration of Sound"; Mendelssohn in his music to "A Midsummer Night's Dream" and his perpetually delightful overtures; Schubert in his songs; Schumann in his "Spring" symphony and his "Forest Scenes" for piano.

But for tonal landscape-painting in its finer estate one must look to the music of the last fifty years—at its best it is peculiarly a modern art. The marvellous increase in expressional efficiency which is the most salient result of the last half-century of musical progress has had no more fortunate issue than the disclosure of means whereby the composer of imagination has been enabled to realise his conceptions with a measure of eloquence undreamed of by his predecessors. The harmonic effects which are to-day at the disposal of any graduate from a conservatory class in composition simply did not exist for Schumann—not to speak of Beethoven or Mozart; for in musical art the innovation of yesterday is the platitude of to-day. Certain forms of musical expression which, when first used by path-breakers like Chopin, Liszt, and Wagner, occasioned shrill protests from the critical conservatives—who alone are timeless and unchanging—have now passed into the common language of the art, and are at the service of any tyro who has learned how to put notes together.

No true analogy for this condition is to be found, as might be supposed, in the case of the poet or the artist, by whom words and pigments may undeniably be manipulated to novel and unexpected ends. In the case of the composer, it is the actual substance of his art which is added to and enriched by the practice of successive generations of creative pioneers. While the artist in words must, in our day, work with virtually the same materials that were used by Keats and Shelley, over whom he has in this respect no fundamental advantage, the contemporary music-maker is very differently circumstanced. He has, at the start, as important an advantage over his predecessor of a century ago as the modern poet would possess if that part of the vocabulary of the English language which is poetically available were unimaginably enlarged by the accretion of a mass of wholly new words, as potent and magical as the old. Mr. Yeats and Mr. Stephen Phillips can, of course, speak of winds and waters with a beauty and an emotion which suffer no impairment from the fact that they are using practically the same verbal materials that were used by Keats and Shelley. But whereas the modern music-maker can speak of winds and waters through the forms of utterance that served Beethoven and Schubert and Schumann, he can also—and herein lies the incalculable superiority of his medium—speak of them in terms that are, in essence, absolutely new. He must still, of course, work within the limits of a few dozen tones of varying pitch; but these correspond, not to the words of language, but to its alphabet; and from this tonal alphabet new words—harmonic and melodic forms—are being evolved with a rapidity and profusion for which in no other kind of æsthetic language is there any comparison. The most uninspired music-wright of to-day can, by the employment of certain harmonic expedients, produce effects which Beethoven would have bartered his soul to be able to achieve. The harmonic effects with which Debussy is enabled to paint the visionary landscape of his "Après-midi d'un Faune"; the wonderful picture of nightfall in upland solitudes which is limned by Vincent d'Indy in his tone-poem, "Jour d'été à la Mon-

tagne"; the malign and dread-enwrapped
landscape which forms the background
of Charles Martin Loeffler's setting of
Verlaine's poem, "Le Son du Cor s'afflige
vers les Bois"; the startlingly vivid chords
which enable MacDowell to suggest the
glittering splendour of this "Wandering
Iceberg": these are concrete examples,
chosen quite at random, of a utilisation
of certain means of musical expression
which not only were undreamt of by the
composers of a century ago, but which
simply did not exist for their utilisation.
They are woven out of a wholly new
tonal stuff, peculiar to our time and use.

It will thus be evident why, as I have
said, it has been possible for musical
landscape-painting to achieve an unexampled pitch of expressiveness within the
last fifty years, and why it is peculiarly
a modern art, an art of our own time.

Since there is everything in Wagner—
the most comprehensive master of musical utterance that the world has yet

known—it is natural that his scores
should contain Nature-painting of an exceptional kind. Wagner ranged freely
over the whole field of human consciousness and experience. He looked into the
heart of man, and wrote, with unequalled
poignancy, of its griefs and joys, its passions and aspirations. He looked, too,
outward upon the created earth, and
he responded lovingly to its multiform phases—its woods, meadows, hills,
streams, gardens; its sunrises and sunsets;
the pageant of the seasons; wind, rain,
mists, storms: he was alive to them all,
and he has celebrated many of their aspects in music that is not merely vivid and
graphic in its pictorial quality, but deeply
poetical and often of superlative beauty.
It would be difficult to parallel in the
whole range of naturalistic tone-painting
the exquisite eloquence and the ravishing
beauty of the music which evokes, as
preparation for the nocturnal meeting of
Tristan and Isolde in King Mark's gar-

den, the spell of that nameless enchantment which the night has ever held for lovers, dreamers, and poets. Nor is it easy to name anything that surpasses such achievements as the picturing of sunlit and tranquil meadows in the "Good Friday Spell" of "Parsifal," or the forest music, storm music, and water music in "The Ring." These are but a few instances of the extraordinary powers of vision and presentment which we find constantly exercised in all of Wagner's essays at Nature-painting.

But though Wagner was the first of those modern composers who have made the art of naturalistic tone-poetry, within the last half-century, a unique and unexampled thing, he was considerably less remarkable as a poet of Nature than as a poet of human emotion, an historian of souls. He speaks with a higher eloquence, a greater power, when he is telling us of the ecstasy of Isolde or the despair of Amfortas, than when he is picturing for us the depths of Siegfried's forest or the majestic flow of the Rhine. He is not pre-eminently a master of musical landscape, fine and memorable as are his excursions in that field.

The supreme achievements of musical landscape-painting are of to-day. We shall find them in the music of four composers of our own time, whose names I have already mentioned, who, by reason of the power and eloquence of their delineation of the natural world, are without peers in their field. They are the Frenchmen Claude Debussy and Vincent d'Indy, and the Americans Charles Martin Loeffler and Edward MacDowell. We shall see these men not only producing Nature-music of incomparable excellence, but approaching their subject-matter from new and unprecedented standpoints.

Wagner, no less than his predecessors among the musical Nature-painters, viewed the outer world quite simply:

either as a congeries of impressive or
lovely subjects to be transcribed upon the
orchestral canvas, or as the cause of certain responsive moods in himself. With
him, as with all of his forerunners in this
field, it was either sheer delineation of external aspects that was attempted, or—as
Beethoven said of his "Pastoral" symphony—an "expression of feeling," of
moods provoked by the contemplation of
Nature under various conditions. Wagner was able to surpass his predecessors in
this kind of writing by reason of his superlative genius as a master of musical
imagery, and also because of the greater
richness, variety, and plasticity of the
medium which he was able to employ—a
medium the enormously increased efficiency of which he himself had done
much to bring about.

When we come to the tonal landscapists who were contemporary with Wagner, or who came after him—such
representative men as (to name but a

few) Raff, Smetana, Rimsky-Korsakoff, Dvorák, Grieg—we find that for the most part they approached Nature in the same spirit as their predecessors: either as a subject to be faithfully rendered, or as the provocator of direct emotional reactions in themselves. But in the landscape-music of those chief contemporary Nature-painters whom I have named— Debussy, d'Indy, Loeffler, and Mac-Dowell—we find different conditions and other aims. Aside from effects secured through the far subtler expressional means which the cumulative enrichment of musical material has enabled them to utilise, we shall find that they disclose an attitude toward their subject-matter—toward the natural world as a theme—which we have not previously encountered among the musical landscapists, though one which is familiar enough in poetic art. For these men the world of external nature is no longer merely a group of phenomena, lovely or terrible,

36

whose picturesque aspects, or the moods which they awaken, are to be sympathetically recorded. It is become rather a kind of magic mirror, throwing back an infinitude of images, entrancing or grotesque, serene or tragic, horrible or sublime—a reflector of the temperaments and prepossessions with which it is confronted. Or—to alter the figure—it is a miraculous harp, an instrument of unlimited range and inexhaustible responsiveness, upon which the performer may improvise at his pleasure. It is Nature made sympathetic and psychical, Nature suffused with subjective emotion. In short, we are witnessing the outcome of that relationship between the susceptible imagination and an infinitely adaptive and compliant Nature which, in literature, resulted in such various poetry as that of Wordsworth, Shelley, Coleridge, Whitman, Poe, Baudelaire, Verlaine. We are no longer in the presence of that natural world which for Couperin,

Haydn, Beethoven, and Mendelssohn, as for Homer and Theocritus, Catullus and Virgil, was in the main an unalterably objective fact—an environing panorama, rather than an enchanted lake in which each observer saw mirrored only the image of his own soul. We have found a condition which, though present in literature for a century, has had no existence in the far less mature art of music before our own day.

In the music of those men whom I have named there are, of course, the widest differences in individual manner of approach—differences so marked as that, for example, which lies between a habit of seeing in the outer world a majestic apparition of the Divine, and the prepossession which finds in it only dark presences and unspeakable omens; but in the art of each we shall find disclosed an attitude which is typical, so far as music is concerned, of our own time.

Claude Debussy is best known to the

world as the composer of "Pelléas et Mélisande," a setting of Maeterlinck's drama in which the musician has swept all the emotional strings and searched the chambers of the heart. But Debussy is more than a subtle psychologist, a writer of poignant spiritual histories; he is also a landscape-painter of an uncommon order. A mercurial being, a protean temperament, he is by turns dramatist, lyrist, rhapsodist, dreamer; Greek, Oriental; a master of line, yet a delicious colorist; a classicist, yet an incorrigible romantic. Yet Debussy is before all else a visionary and mystic, a dweller in the spiritual borderlands. "Our normal, waking, rational consciousness," wrote William James in one of his striking generalisations, "is but one special type of consciousness, whilst all about it, parted from it by the filmiest screens, there lie potential forms of consciousness entirely different." Debussy, having the piercing sight of the mystic, finds no impediment

in these "filmy screens." His usual emotional life is passed on the farther side of
the boundaries of that field of consciousness which most men would call "normal," and he is forever bringing back
across the border rumours of the aspects
and occupations of an unexplored country: tales of fabulous and visionary landscapes; of desires and dreams that come
to fulfilment in some

> " . . . shadowy isle of bliss
> Midmost the beating of the steely sea,"

where he, too, like St. Martin, has seen
"flowers that sounded" and heard "notes
that shone": where, as in the traditions
known to the old Celtic poets, "the noise
of the sunfire on the waves at daybreak is
audible for those who have ears to hear."
That is the world which is native to him.
His music gleams more often with "the
light that never was on sea or land" than
with the light of common day; when it is

most typical, it seems like a precipitation from an authentic world of dreams.

Debussy's nearest kin among landscapists of the brush—with whom he suggests analogies more frequently than with the landscapists of literature—are such differing spirits as Böcklin, Corot, and Whistler. He combines the rich and fantastic imagination of the Swiss and the limpid surfaces of the Frenchman with the American's mastery of *nuance*. But in Debussy these traits are etherealised, alembicated—translated into the terms of that remoter and more aerial region where this singular tone-poet has his essential being. In music there are no analogies to be found for him, save among his imitators. There is in his tonal landscapes no hint of the elemental Nature of Haydn, Beethoven, Wagner, Mendelssohn, Dvorák. His Nature-painting has no smack of the soil, of the solid earth, nothing of the clear outlines, definite forms, and familiar images which we find in the musical scene-painting of the older landscapists. For him, as for Shelley, "Nature is not a picture set for his copying, but a palette set for his brush"; and the colours with which his brush is loaded are such as no painter in tones had ever before employed.

Debussy delights not only in translating into subtle images of tone such familiar phases of the picturesque as reflections in quiet waters and the descending slant of moonbeams, but such less accustomed themes as the stillness of breathless summer noons, the slow procession of the clouds, the mystery of a ruined temple under the moon, the vague melancholy that burdens the distant sound of bells heard through Autumn woods; or, as in his setting of Mallarmé's "Afternoon of a Faun," he conjures before our enamoured eyes a tonal vision the beauty of which seems to have been miraculously recovered from the golden ages of the world: a rhapsodic evocation, of flawless and ravishing loveliness, for which there is no companion-piece in music. Nothing in the least like this transfigured erotic reverie, this exquisite blend of Nature-painting and subtly sensuous lyricism, had ever before been attempted. No one but Debussy could have conceived and accomplished it. But from whatever angle he chooses to transcribe the external world, it is seldom disclosed to his vision save as some enchanted and wonder-breeding apparition. He sees it always as through a necromantic golden mist, which imbues with fantastic light its woods and streams and cloudy turrets, peoples its glades and meadows with strange beings and anonymous presences, and transmits to his ears alluring and mysterious voices.

He is occasionally, it is true, tangible and familiar, as, for example, in his "Rondes de Printemps," No. III of the "Images" for orchestra; but this is one of a very few exceptional cases. Let us, for that reason, consider it a moment.

The piece bears this motto:

"Vive le Mai, bienvenu soit le Mai
Avec son gonfalon sauvage."

But so far as the manifest mood of the music is concerned Debussy might have had in mind the last four of those wonderful lines from Shelley's *Ode to the West Wind*—

" . . . O thou,
Who chariotest to their dark wintry bed
The wingèd seeds, where they lie cold and low,
Each like a corpse within its grave, until
Thine azure sister of the spring shall blow
Her clarion o'er the dreaming earth, and fill
(Driving sweet buds like flocks to feed in air)
With living hues and odours plain and hill."

Let me confess at once that I am aware of no more enchanting celebration of Spring in all music than this thrice-lovable score. Debussy has captured the

44

essential spirit of the Spring, and he has released it in music the vitality, the gayety, the tenderness, the freshness, and the magical charm of which are beyond denotement. These songs of Spring are songs of jubilation. There is in them nothing of the vague but poignant sadness of Spring days—a sadness that can be more intolerable than any sadness that pertains to the moods of Autumn. This music is tremulous with the sense of quickening and stirring life; it is possible to hear in it the merriment of dancing and singing children, or we are reminded of flower-decked creatures sporting in dim forest glades; but its prevailing note is impersonal, elemental. It exhales the vernal rapture of the natural world, rather than the Springtime passion that can fill the human heart with a swelling tide of mysterious joy and unutterable longing. Debussy, when he wrote this delectable and adorable music, sent his spirit into the woods and fields, through

45

gardens and orchards and petal-showered lanes, and out upon the moors and hills; he trod the brown soil of the earth, but he also looked long up into the green branches and the warm gusty sky of May, and savoured the fragrant winds.

Because this music has been grossly undervalued, and occupies a very inconspicuous place among Debussy's larger works, it is worth insisting that the score is a masterpiece. It has remarkable beauties, and it is packed with felicitous and eloquent detail, melodic, harmonic, instrumental. At the first hearing there are passages that for some will perplex the ear, others that will seem to be purposeless or merely wayward; but an increased acquaintance with the score elucidates it completely. It can no more be apprehended at an initial hearing than can any other modern work of novel substance and intricate and subtle texture. But it abundantly rewards continued observation. How lovely, and how saturated with the ineffable charm of Debussy at his best, are the soft staccato chords of the clarinets and flutes near the opening; or the gay dance melody that bursts exuberantly from the strings soon after; or the passage in which the horn sustains a delicate thread of sound above a meditative phrase of the 'cellos; or the indescribable passage for divided strings, *pianissimo;* or that inarticulate whispering and stirring of the whole orchestra which is as the secret processes of the forest made audible; or that passage of entrancing sweetness wherein the violins, high above a soft and rich complexity of supporting tone, carry a tenderly contemplative melody to a pause of quiet and mysterious beauty; and with what unerring, resourceful, and perfect art the music is put upon the orchestra!

It might truly be said of Debussy that in this delectable score, Nature, in the words of Shelley, has indeed made him her lyre.

It will be recalled that the convenient and sufficiently plausible theory of M. Pierre Janet which was mentioned at the beginning of these casual and desultory notes was, in effect, that the typical lover and celebrant of the natural world is characterised by impatience of hampering traditions, by a temperament and a habit of mind essentially anti-conventional. Debussy, one of the most consummate Nature-poets in music, might well have suggested this definition. Those who have reflected sympathetically upon the character of his work need scarcely be told that in his use of suggestive musical symbols he follows a manner of procedure for which there is no exact precedent. He is in this matter, as in all others, a law unto himself. His Nature-music is incomparable not so much because, as Mr. Howells has said of the fiction of Henry James, there is nothing to equal it, "but because there is nothing at all like it." In his depiction of the scenes, moods, processes of Nature, Debussy is hardly ever concerned with achieving a graphic and eloquent representation of the external world. He has an indubitably keen sense of it, but, even in so frank and direct a transcription as the "Rondes de Printemps," he is much less interested in giving us an account of its outward aspects than in recording his perception of what one may call the emotional overtones of the particular spectacle that it discloses to his mind. A poet of unexampled poetic sensitiveness, he is continually aware of surfaces and contours which are not disclosed to his less rarely gifted fellows. He hears with the spiritual ear a strange and haunting music in the wind, a mysterious lilt in "the undersong of the tides," and he knows the streams and woods of an Arcady that is as yet unsung by the poets. Upon the title-page

49

of every one of his essays in tonal landscape-painting (as, indeed, upon all his
music) should be inscribed the cautionary
words of Poe,

"Ah, bear in mind *this* garden is enchanted."

There is some music which should be de-
scribed by poets rather than exposed by
inquisitive æstheticians. Of such is this
magical music of Debussy's.

In his attitude toward the things of
the external world, this master of moods
and visions stands always, as Francis
Thompson has said (not altogether
aptly) of Shelley, "at the very junction
lines of the visible and invisible, and
can shift the points as he wills." But
it is from the remoter position that he ad-
dresses us most often and most engaging-
ly: from that many-coloured land of the
imagination which is known to those,
even the least gifted, for whom the Gates
of Wonder have been opened.

With Debussy's countryman, Vincent

d'Indy, like himself, a musical recusant, we come upon a tonal landscapist of different calibre. He, too, is a mystic; but whereas for Debussy the beauty and wonder of the visible earth are merely so many stimuli to his inflammable and transmuting imagination, for d'Indy they are august revelations of the Divine. He is deeply devout; like Vaughan and Wordsworth, a religious mystic of the purest type. For him the green earth and the majestic canopy of heaven are only, in Wordsworth's phrase, "the garment of God"—an expression of unseen spiritual realities. The spectacle of external Nature, in winsome, forbidding, or awful guise, calls forth in him reverent and exalted emotions. One can conceive him giving Blake's answer to the questioner who asked: "What! when the sun rises do you not see a round disc of fire, something like a guinea?" "No! I see an innumerable company of the heavenly host, cry-ing, 'Holy, Holy, Holy is the Lord God Almighty.' "

For d'Indy the winds and the waters are eloquent of supernal things. The terrible majesty of dawn, the evening light on mountain summits, the peace that falls upon the valley, all discourse to him of divine and immortal things— all are to him, as to that true seer, Jonathan Edwards, "adumbrations of His glory and goodness, of His mildness and gentleness."

It is doubtless a far cry from the austere and excellent Puritan to the exponent of modern musical Paris; yet they view the natural world from fundamentally the same standpoint—the old mystic, who found that "God's excellency, wisdom, purity, and love seemed to appear in everything: in the clouds, the blue sky, in the grass, flowers, trees, in the water, and all nature," and who declared that he was forever "singing forth, with a low voice," his "contemplations of the

Creator"; and the gifted artist of our own time, whose most characteristic achievement, "A Summer Day on the Mountain," is in essence a gravely ecstatic hymn, a tonal pæan in praise of the eternal miracle of created Nature.

His approach to the spectacle of its wonders and beauties is Wordsworthian in its deep and awe-struck reverence and its unrelaxing seriousness and sincerity. He does not, like his younger artistic kinsman, Debussy, see in it all manner of fantastic and mist-enwrapped visions; it is not for him a pageant of delicate and shining dreams—Mallarmé's lazy and indulgent Faun in amorous woodland reverie would not have suggested to him, as to Debussy, music whose sensuousness is as patent as it is marvellously transfigured. The mysticism of d'Indy is preeminently, as I have said, religious; it has no tinge of sensuousness; it is large and austere rather than intimate and impassioned.

D'Indy has written other Nature-music besides the "Jour d'été à la Montagne." There is some in his "Symphonie sur un Air Montagnard Français," and it is the stuff out of which he made his little-known suite for piano, the "Poèmes des Montagnes," an effective and poetic, but not very characteristic outgiving of his younger days. It is the "Jour d'été à la Montagne" which distinguishes him as a Nature-poet,—which puts him in the class of those four transcending landscapists in tone of whose peculiarities as celebrants of the external world I am endeavouring to give some idea. It is because of this one work that I am tempted to think at times that he is the noblest Nature-poet of them all. Indeed, I shall be so bold as to say that by virtue of this score he stands with that great poet of "the Out-world" whom I have already named—Wordsworth.

The "Jour d'été à la Montagne" is a

symphonic poem in three parts, and is representative of d'Indy's mature development as a composer—it was written in 1905. The score is prefaced by a long and rhapsodic prose-poem of Roger de Pampelonne's, which serves to suggest its inspirational basis. Both poem and music are thus divided and entitled: the first part, "Dawn"; the second, "Day (Afternoon Under the Pines)"; the third, "Evening." I shall give in translation a few excerpts from each section as an index to the moods of the piece:

(Dawn): "Awake, dark phantoms! smile to heaven, majestically, for a ray in the Infinite arises and strikes your brow.

"Awake, mountains! The king of space appears!

"Awake, valley! who concealest the happy nests and sleeping cottages; awake singing. And if, in thy chant, sighs also reach me, may the light wind of the morning hours gather them and bear them to God . . . The shadows melt away little by little, before the invading light . . . Laugh or weep, creatures who people this world. Awake, harmonies! God hearkens! . . ."

NATURE IN MUSIC

(Day—Afternoon under the Pines): "How sweet it is to cling to the mountain-sides, broad staircase of heaven! How sweet it is to dream, far from the turmoil of man, in the smiling majesty of the mountain-tops! Here, all earthly sounds mount in harmony towards my rested heart; here, all becomes hymn and prayer . . ."

(Evening): "Night steals across the all-covering sky, and the waning light sends forth a fresh breath swiftly over the weary world. Soon all things sleep beneath the shadows, all appears ghostly in the valley; yet all still lives . . . O Night! Eternal Harmony dwells beneath thy veil; joy and grief are but sleeping. O Night! consuming Life stirs through the all-consuming Day; Life creates itself anew beneath the pearl-strewn mantle of thy outstretched arms . . ."

D'Indy, who has lived much of the time in the mountain regions of his own France, is also, spiritually, a dweller on the heights. In all music (and I speak with anxious sobriety) I am aware of no composer whose thought is more consistently noble, more consistently elevated, than his. Something of the largeness, the upliftedness, the austerity, the strength and sternness of his beloved mountains has decended upon his spirit; so that I cannot conceive him writing music that is ignoble or trivial or meretricious. The "Summer Day on the Mountain" is not only his masterpiece, it is the man himself—a precipitation of his own soul. If none of his scores remained to us but this, we should still be able to reconstruct from it a spiritual image of the essential d'Indy. I have compared him with Wordsworth —and he is, in a remarkable degree, a musical counterpart of Wordsworth the Nature-poet. But he is a Wordsworth of heightened emotional sensibility and more rigid æsthetic scruples. The "Jour d'été" is worthy of Wordsworth at his best. It has an equal aspiration, an equal reverence, an equal raptness and nobility, and it has, besides, an intensity of expression, a distinction of style, which Wordsworth came upon only in rare moments. In this serene and lovely work, the mountains have, for the first time in music, been adequately celebrated. No one who loves the hills, and who is capable of reacting to such music as d'Indy's, can hear this superb hymn without an emotion which will cause him, at least for a while, to look out upon the world with an uplifted heart.

Like much that is fine and rare in the music of our time, this score is years ahead of its contemporaneous public. But when its day shall come, I think that there will be many who cannot fail to listen to it not only with delight in the majestic and tender poetry of its musical speech, but because it will transport them, for a moment, to the heights.

Charles Martin Loeffler, an American of Alsatian birth, Franco-German training, and French affiliations (whose general characteristics as a musician I discuss at length elsewhere in this volume), is, like Debussy and d'Indy, a landscapist of mystical temper, though he lacks the blitheness of the one and the austerity of the other. He is primarily a tragedian, with much of Thomas Hardy's feeling for the ominous and terrible in Nature—indeed, he might not unreasonably be regarded as a living commentary upon that passage of Hardy's concerning Egdon Heath wherein the novelist speaks of those human souls who may come to find themselves "in closer and closer harmony with external things wearing a sombreness distasteful to our race when it was young." Loeffler betrays this instinctive sympathy with the tragical in Nature. His spiritual brethren are Poe, Baudelaire, Maeterlinck, Verlaine, in their darker and disconsolate hours. In the mood which is most frequent with him, he is native to a world oppressed by nameless and immemorial griefs, dolorous with the shadow of death, where the winds are heavy with bodement and vague menace. Images of the King of Terrors haunt his imagination; a vast and bitter melancholy encompasses him.

NATURE IN MUSIC

Thus he is drawn to contrive tonal analogues for such a desolate and sinister landscape as he has found in Maurice Rollinat's dire poem, "The Pool," with its mordant picturing of dank and lonely marshes, lowering twilight skies, complaining frogs, and the vacuous, spectral face of the moon. He has sought musical expression also for Rollinat's other and yet more woful picture of the ghostly bagpipe-player whose groaning tune is heard by night, under a bleak sky, "near the cross-roads of the crucifix"; and among his smaller pieces there is none more characteristic than his superb setting of Verlaine's unutterably mournful fantasy of sobbing horn notes borne at sunset upon Winter winds—"Le Son du Cor s'afflige vers les Bois."

He can paint, it is true, in other colors. His orchestral transcription of the exquisite aubade which Verlaine, in "La Bonne Chanson," addressed to his bride, is music of such enchanting freshness, sweetness, and lyric rapture that it recalls the saying of Whitman: "What subtle tie is this between one's soul and the break of day?" But in his nature-painting we find for the most part canvases of sable hue: landscapes upon which the sun has forever set, situate in some "dim empire of sorrow," where—as in the grievous fantasy of wailing horn tones which he has paraphrased —"all the air is like an autumn sigh."

We encounter a temperament of a different order in the American, Edward MacDowell. MacDowell was a landscapist who would have compelled the delighted attention of Matthew Arnold, had that sensitive gauger of poetic values been as responsive to musical as to literary influences. MacDowell was, strangely enough, the only Celt who has ever written music of first-rate quality; and he was also the only valid exponent of Celtic feeling and Celtic perception that is to be found in the whole range of what we call "artistic" music, as distinguished from folk-music. Though an American by birth, he was a Celt by virtue of ancestry and innate affiliation, and he enjoyed that deep and abiding intimacy with natural things which is the incontestable heritage of the Celt. He was tenderly and acutely aware of every phase and alteration of the earth, sea, and sky. To him, as to Richard Feverel, the fields and the waters "shouted to him golden shouts." He had Keats's delight in the sheer actuality and presence of the natural world. He was halted by the echo of the wind along the shore, the aromatic breath of the woods, the smell of the warm turf, the colour and bloom and opulence of Nature in her immediate and elemental appeal. To such varied persuasions as these he responded with exceptional quickness and intensity, and he knew how to capture and convey the sense of them in music which, regarded as sheer Nature-painting, stands alone in the intimacy and vividness of its rendering.

But there was another and more notable side to his relations with the outer world. He had the Celt's peculiar and instinctive sensibility toward the appeal of that which is remote, solitary, of strange beauty and import—the imaginative leaning toward "old, forgotten, far-off things," and the wistful sadness in the contemplation of them, which sets the Celt, as an artist, definitely apart. Above all, he had that distinctively Celtic way of transcribing Nature which Arnold has called "magical." Those are the chief, the distinguishing, possessions of his Nature-music when it is most typical; the feeling of the remote and irreclaimable which underlies and pervades it; and the magical power with which that feeling is expressed and communicated. He can achieve, as I have said, vivid similes of near and familiar things: the flavour of woods, fields, gardens, the brooding mystery of deep woods, the wide, tonic spaces of moor and sky. But what is unique and unparalleled in his music is its quality of Celtic magic, which touches and transfigures even his frankest rendering of the sunlit scenery of the accustomed world; though it is never so seizing as when it carries the rumour of some wild Ossianic night, "when the Gael-strains chant themselves from the mists"; or when—and perhaps, then, most poignantly—its burden is "the ancient sorrow of the hills."

There is another aspect of tonal Nature-painting which it is worth while to consider. It is that which might be sufficiently indicated in a distinction between musical landscape-painting and musical geography; and I shall revert, for convenience, to the music of Claude Debussy to point this distinction—in particular, I shall allege his orchestral suite, "Ibéria" (the second section of the set of

"Images" of which "Rondes de Printemps" is the third).

Debussy, in these impressions of what Mr. James would call "the Spanish scene" (the suite is in three parts: (1) "Par les rues et par les chemins"; (2) "Les parfums de la nuit"; (3) "Le matin d'un jour de fête"), turned, for a moment, from the field of musical landscape to the field of musical geography—an unfortunate departure. It is comparatively easy to set geography to music—to evoke, by means of characteristic rhythms, melodics, and instrumental colours, definite impressions of particular countries, regions, and peoples. The thing has, of course, been done again and again in music; for Spain it has been done with especial effectiveness by Bizet, Chabrier, Ravel, to name but a few. But how often has it yielded music that has any higher quality than picturesqueness? It is not easy to think of a single example of music geographically inspired that bears the stamp of the high-est musical eloquence. The immediate and stimulating need of being "picturesque" and nationally or racially veracious supersedes the familiar and less exciting need of persuading the heart by eloquent speech. I do not know of any music whose motive springs from the desire for geographical celebration rather than from the contemplation of abstract Nature which is more than skin-deep in its emotional quality and more than external in its charm. Such music at its best is fascinating, engrossing, delightful; but does it ever possess the imagination and conquer the emotions as does sheer musical landscape-painting? Set the brilliant and undeniably captivating "Spanish Rhapsody" of Chabrier beside d'Indy's "Summer Day on the Mountain"; set Charpentier's "Impressions of Italy" beside Loeffler's "The Pool"; set Debussy's "Ibéria" beside his "Rondes de Printemps": which makes

66

the profounder address to the imagination: the vivid and faithful representation of geographic traits—the communication of a particular atmosphere and environment; or the suggestion of a mood or aspect of Nature which has no specific relation to the map? D'Indy's mountain under various Summer aspects might be in the Tyrol or in New Hampshire; Loeffler's pool might be in Normandy or in Massachusetts; the Springtime landscape of which Debussy sings might be in England, or in Brittany, or in Bohemia, or it might be visible from the window of the dweller in a New Jersey suburb. To write music that aims to be specifically and definitely local is necessarily to commit oneself to the employment of rhythms, melodic forms, orchestral colors, that may or may not be congenial to one's own habit of artistic speech; their employment is almost inevitably a *tour de force,* rather than a spontaneous utterance of personal vision and emotion. To write with the deliberate intention of suggesting a particular section of the map is to bind oneself to more or less rigid formulas. If you would impart a sense of Spain you are bound to employ certain dance rhythms, certain instrumenal timbres, which are as inevitable in any tonal representation of Spain as are the tourist cap, the monocle, and the gaiters in the costume of the stage Englishman of ancient farce. They are expected and inescapable; and as not every composer who elects to tell us of Spain is suited by natural affinity to employ happily the musical idioms that are associated with it, there is nothing surprising in the fact that he should produce music which interests and entertains us as an exercise, relatively successful or futile, rather than persuades us as an expression of some profound and individual conviction of the loveliness or the majesty or the pathos of the natural world—the natural world that is outside the influence of manners and customs and boundary-lines. Nor does it follow that when the composer is native to the country which he chooses to portray, music of first-class quality will result; the more he limits the sources of his inspiration, the more he limits its power, its depth, and its range of appeal.

"Ibéria" is, indisputably, an amazing *tour de force*. Debussy had never before been so venturesome in harmony, so resourceful in rhythm, so original and untrammelled in melodic thought. This last statement will perhaps be incomprehensible to those who insist that Debussy is not only "lacking in rhythm," but that he is barren of melody. The truth is, of course, as every sensitive and receptive student of Debussy knows, that his remarkable scores are singularly fertile in rhythmic and melodic ideas—only they are very different ideas from those to which Schubert and Wagner and Chopin and Brahms have accustomed us: so different, indeed, so new and strange, that the observer of conventional taste and standards makes the time-honoured mistake of denying that they are there at all. Debussy does not write the kind of rhythm or the kind of melody, any more than he writes the kind of harmony, with which the average observer is familiar in Chopin and Wagner, Grieg and Puccini; *ergo,* his harmony is insane, his melody non-existent, his rhythm to seek. There are ideas of extraordinary originality in "Ibéria." But, because, as I believe, of the fetters which he placed upon his inspiration when he chose his subject, these ideas have not the eloquence that Debussy, when his thought is unshackled, knows how to command. There is nothing in this score, as I have said, that is worthy to be set beside page after page of "Rondes de Printemps." Yet the music is remarkable in many ways. Its rhythmic variety is astonishing; the melodic thought is often of rare subtlety; there is harmonic invention that never flags, that never says the otiose or quotidian thing; and the orchestration is ingenious, dazzling, masterly. The first movement, "Par les Rues et Par les Chemins," a picture full of colour and animation, is the longest and the most elaborate, occupying fifty-three of the hundred and eight pages which comprise the score. This movement is the most energetic piece of orchestral writing that we have had from Debussy; and it is also the most concrete and definite in imagination. It moves close to the ground; it is concerned with the sights and sounds and colours of familiar life, as they are to be observed in their Spanish setting. And this is true also of the third and much shorter movement, "Le matin d'un Jour de Fête." The finer Debussy—finer, because he is here concerned with Nature rather than geography—emerges in the middle movement, "Les Parfums de la Nuit," a night-picture full of voluptuous

71

and romantic beauty. There are passages
in it which are very nearly Debussy at his
best—as that in which the languorous
song of the oboe is heard above synco-
pated chords (*"expressif et pénétrant,"* as
the composer has marked them) in the
divided strings: a melody of long breath
and enchanting tenderness. And this, one
may venture to observe—*pace* the dis-
senters—is an authentic melody, though
it is perhaps not the kind that Puccini, or
Massenet, or Mr. Victor Herbert, would
have chosen to write.

But this brilliant piece of geographical
denotement has none of the magical freshness, the irresistible loveliness, of "Rondes
de Printemps"; it has none of the ravishing spontaneity, the perfect grace and
fluidity of movement, of that incomparable pæan in praise of the exquisite
ardours of Spring and the vernal earth.
In "Ibéria" he is merely doing, with extraordinary brilliancy and *élan*, the sort
of thing which many can do with success

and some few with mastery, though none with quite the invention and manipulative ease that he displays. But in "Rondes de Printemps," in the "Après-midi," in the Nature-pieces for piano wherein he is unaware of the cartographer, of boundaries and manners and customs: when, in short, he is moving in a region where he is sovereign and unique, there is no one who can throw upon the orchestral canvas such gleaming and enchanted landscapes, such rhapsodic yet luminous and delicate transcriptions of Nature, as this master-builder of vaporous and phantasmal worlds.

MUSIC AND THE SEA

"The sea . . . the very words even have magic. It is like the sound of a horn in woods, . . . like the cry of wind leaping the long bastions of silence. To many of us there is no call like it, no other such clarion of gladness."—*Fiona Macleod.*

In a strange and touching book by a little-known mystic there is recounted a

singular fable of the Celts concerning
Manannan, god of the sea and the winds.
Lying beside the shore of the sea, Manannan overheard a man and woman talking
together. "He heard the man offer to
the woman love and home and peace.
And the woman, who was a creature of
the sea (or, as some say, a sea-woman),
answered him, saying that she would
bring to him 'the homelessness of the sea,
and the peace of the restless waves, and
love like the wandering wind.' Then the
man rebuked her, saying that she could
be no woman; whereupon she laughed
and entered the water. When she had
vanished, Manannan appeared to the
man in the guise of a youth, and ques-
tioned him concerning his love for the
sea-woman. He then proffered him ad-
vice, bidding him seek a young girl whom
he would meet singing on the heather,
one who would be white and fair. But
for consolation, because of the man's lost
love in the water, Manannan told him

74

that he would give him a gift; and he took a wave of the sea and threw it into the man's heart. The man did as he was bid, wedding and dying and leaving children after him. But a mysterious thing befell; for he and his children and his children's children knew by day and by night a love that was tameless and changeable as the wandering wind, and a longing that was unquiet as the restless wave, and the homelessness of the sea. And that is why they are called *Sliochd - na - mara,* the Clan of the Waters."

It sometimes fantastically seems as if only those who are in an interior sense children of the sea, who are attuned to what Mr. Kipling has called its "excellent loneliness" through some secret intimacy of the spirit, can capture its spell and imprison it in forms of beautiful art. Many poets have sung of the sea, have listened enthralled to its multifarious voice; yet how many have rendered,

through any sustained and ample vision,
a full and eloquent impression of it?
When one recalls that the supreme Eliza-
bethan achieved such a phrase as

"in cradle of the rude imperious surge";

when one thinks of

"the unplumbed, salt, estranging sea"

of Arnold; or of Swinburne's wonderful line,

"the deep divine dark dayshine of the sea,"

it becomes apparent that to poets of very
diverse capacities has it been given to
illuminate by gleams this vast and subtle
theme. But those masters of poetic
speech whom one thinks of as having
known long and revealing communion
with the sea: do they not seem to have
in their blood—to adopt the mystical no-
tion of the ancient legend of the north
—the restless and vital pulse of the sea?

NATURE IN MUSIC

It is not unilluminating to think of Swinburne, in whose verse the movement and colour of the sea are so triumphantly pervasive, as of the children of the wave; or of Whitman, with his cosmic chantings of the vastness and mystery of the deep, as of the clan of the waters.

At the best, the poet who would undertake to convey any image of the sea by means of words is hampered by his vehicle. It is not necessarily to hold a brief for the art of music to feel that the medium of tones is incomparably fitted for rendering impressions of the sea. The analogies are as obvious as they are beguiling: there is nothing in the visible pageant of the natural world that is more completely the embodiment of movement, of rhythmic life, than the sea; nothing that is so infinitely various in its enchantment; and music, pre-eminently among the arts, can convey the sense of movement—not alone the quality of movement that is irresistible and impelling, but the subtler dynamic life that stirs almost imperceptibly under quiet surfaces; and it is the most flexible and plastic of the arts.

It would seem, then, as if the sea must have been for the music-maker a continuous inspiration; yet one will search among the pages of the masters of three centuries of instrumental music—a period which covers almost its entire life—without finding more than a dozen important examples of what may be called marine tone-painting; and these are all virtually of our own day.

The case, though, is not so mysterious as it seems. To begin with, it is clear that the tone-poet who would attempt a seascape of even small dimensions must have at his command an instrument of great power, richness, and variety of expression. Such a vehicle of expression did not exist prior to the second quarter of the nineteenth century. An imaginative composer who, in the day of Johann

NATURE IN MUSIC

Sebastian Bach, let us say, should have endeavoured to convey some tonal impression of the sea in one of its majestic, alluring, or sinister moods, would have been in as embarrassing a situation as a painter who should attempt a seascape with an equipment consisting of a tube of black and a tube of red paint and a brush with half a dozen bristles, or as Mr. Swinburne would have been had his vocabulary been limited to that of a schoolboy of sixteen. Our supposititious eighteenth-century composer would, in other words, have lacked the necessary tools. The orchestra of his day was a poor and thin affair, deficient in number and variety of instruments; and instead of the full-voiced pianoforte of our time he had nothing more expressive at his command than the gracious tinkling of harpsichords and spinets.

The orchestra as we know it—an instrument of expression that is almost unrivalled in range and eloquence—is a heritage from Richard Wagner, who in his turn had received valuable suggestions from the experiments of that tumultuous Romantic, Hector Berlioz. The modern orchestra, therefore, and the modern manner of using it—for the technic of orchestration has steadily kept pace with the growth of the orchestra itself—are both matters of very recent history; Berlioz has been dead less than half a century, and the magician of "Tristan" and the "Ring" only a generation. Nor has that other eloquent medium of the contemporary tone-poet, the pianoforte, disclosed its full possibilities of utterance save within the last few decades. The vivid and delicate effects of colour, the rich perspectives, the superb sonorities which are familiar to us in the piano music of Brahms, Grieg, MacDowell, Debussy, would have been both technically and mechanically impossible in the day which saw the birth of the Beethoven Sonata.

NATURE IN MUSIC

It will be seen, then, that only within recent years has the composer of imaginative and pictorial instinct had at his disposal adequate means for the conveyance of his thought. Evidently for any considerable music of the sea we must look to the moderns, to the men of the last half-century—the writers of "programme music," the tone-poets and tone-painters, the realists and impressionists: those who have made of music an articulate and expressive art, a medium of dramatic and poetical utterance, rather than an art of pure design. Yet even in modern music, and despite the means now at their disposal, there have been comparatively few music-makers who have, in Ossian's phrase, "gone the seaward way." Musical art, from the time of the first realists, has had, as we have already seen, an abundance of landscapists, crude and meagre in achievement as, in the earlier days, they necessarily were. But one cannot help wondering at the comparative rarity in musical history of the tone-poet of the sea. Doubtless, as it was said at the beginning of these remarks, the tribe of the wave are necessarily few in numbers. The sea is not for all, nor even for the truly imaginative, a thing compact of enthralment, an alluring presence—not all could speak of "the many-twinkling smile of ocean." There are those whom it repels, for whom the sense of its vast loneliness, its unconquerable mystery, is barren of any enkindling effect upon the spirit: there are many who might ask, "Who hath desired the sea?" Not for all is the sea exhilarating and arousing. It has its own clan, those who are subtly bound to it through some unfathomable affinity, who will always respond to its exultant or secret call—in whose souls is

"the sense of all the sea."

But these are few. Some among them

are poets or dreamers; but not many, even of these, work through the medium of the difficult and forbidding art of music; nor, alas! have all the musical seascapists been either poetic or imaginative.

One should think first, perhaps (I have no intention of pursuing an exhaustive inquiry in this desultory paper), of Mendelssohn, in recalling the earliest musical sea-painting which still falls persuasively upon the modern sense. In his gently picturesque and fanciful overtures, "The Hebrides," "The Lovely Melusina," and "Becalmed at Sea and Prosperous Voyage" (after Goethe's little poems, "Meerestille" and "Glückliche Fahrt"), there is marine painting of a kind which to-day seems somewhat lean in poetic quality, despite its indisputable grace; though it should be recalled that Richard Wagner, on the strength of certain effects in the "Hebrides" overture, acclaimed its composer as a nature-painter of the first order—praise which could not have sounded as extravagant when it was spoken as it does in our own time.

Rubinstein in his "Ocean" symphony painted upon a far larger canvas, and with a richer palette, than did the precise and conservative author of the "Hebrides" score. When Rubinstein composed music he wrote always out of a full heart; his moods and his emotions were incomparably more intense and more contagious than were those of the thinner-blooded Mendelssohn; but his deficiency was, ultimately, the same: he lacked the power of creating musical ideas—harmonic, melodic, rhythmical concepts—of importance and enduring vitality. There is an oppressive pathos in his "Ocean" symphony, his most ambitious and significant work. One feels, in listening to its plethoric measures—the score is immense in extent—the sadness which always attends a piece of creative art wherein the inspiring impulse has failed to fructify in shapes of beauty.

NATURE IN MUSIC

Yet Rubinstein, it is clear, was deeply stirred by the sea—especially the sea in its majestic aspect. The rapture of it, the fascination of its more joyous moods, are not in his music; yet within the often commonplace exterior of this score there has been distilled something of the authentic spirit of the ocean in its graver condition—one hears at times the huge and solemn voice of the sea, chanting its immemorial song under lonely skies.

There are in the Wagner operas fragments of sea-music which revive one's persistent regret that the inventor of the modern lyric drama did not write more for the orchestra alone and less for the stage. There is some splendid tone-painting of the sea in its most tragic and turbulent moods in the overture to "The Flying Dutchman"; and there are a few delectable touches of the same graphic delineation in "Tristan and Isolde." The Russians—Tchaikovsky, Rimsky-Korsakoff, Glazounoff, Rachmaninoff—have essayed, with varying success, to fix upon the symphonic canvas something of the spell of deep waters; there is sea-music of a not too imposing quality in symphonic poems by the Belgian, Paul Gilson, the American, John Knowles Paine, and the German, Max Schillings; and for the voice in combination with instruments there is a quantity of sea-music more or less negligible. But until that true and lamented genius, Edward MacDowell, put forth, ten years before his death, his volume of "Sea Pieces" for the piano, it is not too much to say that the ocean as a theme for the modern tone-poet had not achieved any searchingly eloquent expression.

The wonder of these eight short piano pieces, most of which are less than four pages in length, is that, within an incredibly brief compass, and with only the monochromatic keyboard of the piano for their medium, they present a composite picture of the sea that is astonishing in its variety and breadth. Here is genuine sea-poetry—poetry to match with that of Whitman and the author of "Thalassius" and "A Channel Passage." The music is drenched with salt spray, wind-swept, exhilarating; there are pages in it through which rings the thunderous laughter of the sea in its moments of cosmic and terrifying elation, and there are pages through which drift sun-painted mists, or wherein the ineffable tenderness of the ocean under Summer stars is conveyed with a beauty that is both magical and deep. The range of mood is in itself singularly impressive, passing from the superb exordium, an apostrophe "To The Sea," to the melting and solemn loveliness of "Starlight"; from "In Mid-Ocean"—where the thought is of Whitman's sea of

"brooding scowl and murk"—

to the ominous and unquiet grandeur of

NATURE IN MUSIC

"From the Depths,"—where again one recalls the sea of Whitman, speaking

"... with husky, haughty lips."

These remarkable pieces, which are not yet either adequately known or appraised, are epics in little—and the littleness, it should be noted, is wholly a quantitative matter: their spiritual and imaginative reach is not easily to be measured.

It has been left, though, for the most original of contemporary music-makers, Claude Debussy, to throw upon the spacious canvas of the modern orchestra a tonal picture of the sea that is commensurate both in dimensions and inspiration with the most notable seascapes in literature and painting. Debussy is, as we all know, at once an iconoclast and a path-breaker. He has displayed a serene indifference toward many of the sacrosanct canons of the orthodox musician,

and he has created a form of his own,
evolving through the processes of a swift
and liberating inspiration a uniquely fluid
and untrammelled style. He is also, as
we have noted in considering his achievements as a musical landscapist, a dreamer, a mystic, and a man of subtle and
clairvoyant imagination. Now it is fair-
ly obvious that such a musician was pre-
destined to paint the sea, and in a manner
the reverse of ordinary. It will soon be
superfluous to praise, as I have praised in
the foregoing pages of these casual and
rambling remarks, such things as his orchestral setting of Mallarmé's ecstatic
reverie, "The Afternoon of a Faun"—
music that is like an iridescent web of
fire and dew; his exquisite "Nocturnes"
(in one of which, "Sirens," there is a
delicious limning of moonlit waters) ; his
"Rondes de Printemps"; his landscape
impressions for the piano. But it will
be long before he is adequately praised
for the least liked, yet, as some have

thought, the largest and noblest, of his symphonic utterances: his orchestral "sketches" (as he calls them), "La Mer" —the most extraordinary sea-music that has ever crystallized into tone.

Debussy has what Sir Thomas Browne would have called "a solitary and retired imagination." He has viewed the multiform spectacle of the sea with the preternaturally sharpened vision of the mystic—a mystic who is both a poet and a painter; and it will have been observed throughout these remarks that both our landscapists and our seascapists in music have been viewed interchangeably as poets and painters—for such, at will, they are. So, here, when Debussy assumes to depict in his music such things as "dawn and noon on the ocean," "sport of the waves," and a "dialogue of the wind and the sea," he is at once poet and painter, but he is also something more: he is a spiritual mystic. It is not chiefly of these things that he is telling us, but of

the changing phases of a sea of dreams,
a chimerical sea, a thing of strange visions and stranger voices, of fantastic
colours and incalculable winds—a phan-
tasmagoria of the spirit, rife with evanes-
cent shapes and presences that are at
times full of bodement and vague terror,
at times lovely and infinitely capricious,
at times sunlit and dazzling. Yet beneath these elusive and impalpable overtones the reality of the living sea persists:
the immemorial enchantment lures and
enthralls and terrifies; so that we come to
wonder if the two are not, after all,
identical—the sea that seems an actuality of brine and tossing spray and inexorable depths and reaches, and that remoter sea, that uncharted and haunted
and incredible sea, that opens before the
magic casements of the dreaming mind.

II

DEATH AND THE MUSICIANS

DEATH AND THE MUSICIANS

The poets have spoken nobly of death;
but in music the idea of death has not
been a wonted theme; and how many
composers, in their occasional disserta-
tions upon the subject, have discoursed
of it with nobility, with exaltation, with
spiritual valour? The query is an engrossing one for those who are minded to re-
flect upon the relation between the art
of music and the inner life of man. When
Sergei Vassilievitch Rachmaninoff, the
sombre-souled Russian music-maker,
composed his symphonic poem, "The
Island of the Dead," after the remarkable painting of Arnold Böcklin, he made
a deliberate attempt to do what has seldom been essayed in music—he sought to
expose in tones a conception of the idea
of death.

Böcklin's picture, of which there are several variants, is well known. The Swiss painter might have taken for its motto the opening lines of the sonnet of Thomas Hood:

"There is a silence where hath been no sound;
There is a silence where no sound may be."

Indeed, Böcklin is said to have remarked of his picture that "it must produce such an effect of stillness that any one would be frightened to hear a knock on the door." The lonely, sunless island, awful in its solitude and its solemnity, with its frowning cliffs and mournful cypress-trees, rising out of a windless sea; the boat that is slowly nearing the harbour with its cargo, the garlanded coffin and the white-robed, anonymous figure; the utter lifelessness and isolation, the unending silence, of this desolate kingdom of shadows—what music-maker of imagination, attracted by Böcklin's sombre fantasy, could fail to be moved by these things to eloquent, or at least sympathetic, utterance?

Rachmaninoff is a tone-poet of imagination. He demonstrated that fact in his earlier orchestral picture, "The Cliff" (after a poem by Lermontoff)—a piece of tonal delineation, half landscape and half seascape, of extraordinary breadth and power. Böcklin's painting has stirred him to a greater depth, and to finer issues. He has done more than translate into tone the pictorial substance and the mood of the picture; he is in this music both scene-painter and psychologist. He paints for us the unruffled sea, the solemn approach of the barge with its quiet passengers, the dark and mysterious haven which it nears. But he has done more: he has given us, as it were, the emotional background of the picture. He discerns its mortal complement. He remembers the grief, the lamentation, the loneliness of those who still are of the world—who have not yet taken passage

upon that uncharted sea with that un-
hastening ferryman: he remembers "the
measureless waters of human tears."

His music is thus not only a faithful
commentary upon the picture, but an am-
plification of its idea. He has enlarged
upon his text, though he has told us nothing which was not implicit in it. He has
said more than Böcklin has said, but nothing that Böcklin did not connote. His
subject, indeed, gave him neither oppor-
tunity nor excuse for saying anything in a
different key. Böcklin's vision is a fundamentally despondent, a fundamentally
unillumined one. The musician could
not justifiably, even if he had cared to,
impose a different hue upon it. He has
expatiated with beauty and feeling upon
the theme which he chose; if his discussion of it lacks exaltation and nobility
we must blame his choice, not his power
of discourse. There is no aspiration, no
elevation, in the music; there is none in
the picture.

NATURE IN MUSIC

In this work of Rachmaninoff's, therefore, we find an example of that conception of death which is the prevailing
conception with those music-makers
who have concerned themselves with
thoughts of the event which waits
upon mortality, and who have deliberately turned their meditations into musical utterance. The poets, admittedly,
have dwelt nobly upon the thought of
death. Disregarding the conventional
literature of consolation, we may trace
backward for thirty centuries the steps
of those who have walked "the small old
path the seers knew," and who have
strewn it thick with the testations of an
illumined spiritual vision. But music
contains few such inspired visions, apart
from the music of the church. The tone-
poets, when they have discoursed of
death, have not often, with Omar, sent
their souls into the invisible; when they
have brooded upon death they have, for
the most part, brooded upon it in melan-

choly or despair; they have been most
seizing and memorable as artists when
they have been most completely earth-
bound as philosophers. They have generally fastened their minds upon that
grief and lamentation which are the
human ministers of the Dark Angel; or
they have bent despairing or mournfully
submissive eyes upon the River of Forget-
fulness, reciting, in chants that are often
of immortal beauty, "Matter is conqueror—matter, triumphant only, con-
tinues onward." When they have sent
their gaze beyond the open grave it has
been only to shrink from the thought of
that unknown region which, in one of his
infrequent "downcast hours," the most
valiant of modern seers has dolorously
apprehended: "where neither ground is
for the feet nor any path to follow, . . .
no map there, nor guide, nor voice sounding, nor touch of human hand, . . . nor
lips, nor eyes, are in that land."

What the music-maker is most apt to

produce when he meditates upon death
are such threnodies as we have had from
those two master elegists of the tone-art
—Chopin and Tchaikovsky; and the Russian typifies the more characteristically
that point of view which has been alleged.
Upon the music of Tchaikovsky (and
this applies not alone, though chiefly,
to the "Pathetic" Symphony) the rumour of our mortality casts always
a menacing shadow, even though at
times it seems almost wholly absent.
The note of which he is the most perfect
master is the note of lamentation; and he
is only completely himself when he is
sounding that note. For Tchaikovsky
dreaded with passionate protest what Sir
Thomas Browne called "the iniquity of
oblivion." He feared the thought of
death with a shuddering and poignant
terror; and into his most sincere and
characteristic deliverance, the "Pathetic"
Symphony (though not only there), he
emptied all the dark troubles of his heart

—all that he knew of anguished apprehension and foreboding, of grief that is unassuageable, of consternation and despair. Tchaikovsky never divulged the meaning of this incomparably touching music, but its purport is unmistakable. Its burden is the finality of death—the eternal oblivion and silence of the grave; and its hopelessness is as manifest and indisputable as it is utter and unrelieved. He has not here incurred the calm reproach of Krishna: "Thou hast grieved for those who need no grief"; for his grief is rather for himself—for the precious things of the world which he sees slipping irreclaimably from his grasp; for the tragedies and frustrations of his own life. This music—infinitely affecting, at times of an almost insupportable pathos: in many ways a wonderful, a unique, score—this music is saturated with the particular emotion which moved Edgar Allan Poe when he wrote his heartbroken "Dream Within a Dream":

> "I stand amid the roar
> Of a surf-tormented shore,
> And I hold within my hand
> Grains of the golden sand:
> How few! Yet how they creep
> Through my fingers to the deep,
> While I weep, while I weep!
> O God! can I not grasp
> Them with a tighter clasp?
> O God! can I not save
> One from the pitiless wave?
> Is all that we see or seem
> But a dream within a dream?"

But though Tchaikovsky is the typical tone-poet of death, there is not lacking in the music of certain other men a note very different from the note which he most persistently sounds. None of the mystical poets has spoken with a more serene nobility of death than has Schubert in his "Death and the Maiden"; nor will one find in the most ecstatic meditations of those seers and prophets

who have beheld supernal visions a more
sublimated hymn to death than that
which Wagner, arch-transcendentalist
and mystic, has given us in the transfigured music of Isolde's "Liebestod"—music of pure spiritual ecstasy, whose won-
drous exaltation of mood could have
sprung from no other source but Wagner's profound intuition of the luminous
wisdom of the East. Nor, again, has
poetry a more elevated word to say of
death than has Richard Strauss in that
noblest of his tone-poems, "Death and
Transfiguration."

No one, I think, would be far wrong
in saying that we have in these three
widely dissimilar though fundamentally
related works the most spiritually en-
nobled and valorous declarations which
music has yet given us upon the essential
theme of death—of death, that is to say,
as a condition rather than an event. In
the "Tod und das Mädchen" of Schubert,
the "Liebestod" of Wagner, the "Tod

und Verklärung" of Strauss, we have the record, as it were, of visions which beheld death as an accomplishment either of peace, or ecstasy, or fulfilment; but in each there is the revelation of a thing attained; and in each is the signature of a high spiritual intuition. In each the music (if not the composer) conveys the serene rebuke of Socrates unto Glaucon: "Are you not aware that the soul is immortal and imperishable?"

The several visions differ widely in character and intensity. The figure of Death in Schubert's wonderful song is a being of supreme benignity—we think (even though we must make a transposition of sex to do so) of Whitman's "dark mother always gliding near with soft feet"; and of the strangely similar, though sublimer, "great mother" of the Katha Upanishad—the "great mother full of divinity, who comes forth through life, standing hid in secret." In the glorious rhapsody of Isolde we have music which

is as a commentary upon the words of the
Master to Sâuryâyanin Gârgya: "And
when he is rapt by the radiance, the bright
one no longer sees dreams. Then within
him the bliss arises." While the majestic
and plangent conception of Strauss again
recalls an evocative phrase of Whitman,
unwearying prophet of spiritual resurrec-
tions: "the superb vistas of death." There
are such vistas in this tone-poem of
Strauss's.

But there is room for a finer and loftier
word upon death than has yet been said
in music—a word which music is pre-
eminently fitted to convey. The inspiration for it is to be found in the unnum-
bered messages of the profounder seers
as they are luminously recorded in the
books of the world's wisdom, from the
Bhagavad Gita to Plato, from the Apocalypse to the seers and dreamers of to-
day. "There is no answer in words,"
says a sage and clairvoyant mystic of our
own time, "to the question, What is the

great Beyond? nor can there be." That, indeed, concerns those things that cannot be named. Yet music, whose prime function it is to transcend words, to supersede concrete expression, can sometimes work this miracle, and can communicate a sense of nameless and unutterable things. And so, perhaps, it may yet speak that finer and loftier word upon death for which we have wished—a word which shall convey the reality of a vision joyous yet serene, of infinite felicity and ineffable peace. It will be spoken, let us predict, by one who has "crossed over all the sorrows of the heart," and who has found that path which stretches far away, by which go "the Seers who know the Eternal"; and he will have brooded' upon the words of that revelation that was made to Nachiketas in the ancient Books of Wisdom—that revelation which celebrates "the resting-place of the world, the endlessness of desire, the shore where there is no fear, greatly praised, and the wide-sung resting-place." Or he may look only into his own soul, and may thus come to know the truth as simply as it became known to little Tyltyl and Mytyl during their search for the Blue Bird, in that scene of inexpressible and tender sublimitỳ where they seek him among the dead in the graveyard; for when, obeying Tyltyl's magic command, the mounds open and the graves gape wide, the lifting vapours reveal only a garden of flowering lilies.

"Where are the dead?" asks Mytyl, in bewilderment.

"There *are* no dead," answers Tyltyl.

III

STRAUSS AND THE GREEKS

STRAUSS AND THE GREEKS

There are some who, noting the recurrent pother stirred up by the compositions of Richard Strauss, may remember the words of Socrates to the Athenians: "You are vexed, as drowsy persons are when they are awakened." Surely Strauss is unequalled in all music as an awakener! Whatever may be justly said in detraction of him—and he is full of faults—it cannot be denied that he always stirs the waters. The commotion may bring up something rare and precious, or it may bring up mud; but the activity is indisputable. He is the most dynamic, the most inveterately alive, of all music-makers. For sheer energy there is no one to set beside him. He is often irritating—and he irritates by his banality and triviality no less than

by his staggeringly complacent habit of
writing music that seemingly has
neither point nor coherence, neither
reason nor logic. But to be indifferent to his address is impossible. He
can be commonplace with a bla-
tancy that sets the teeth on edge. He
can achieve a degree of bad taste that
passes credibility. His *gamineries* are
unpardonable. He can offend and exasperate with a cool effrontery that is almost engaging. He can be as trivial as
Bellini, as sentimental as Gounod, as
pompously empty as Meyerbeer. He is
the most reckless, the most untamed, the
most preposterous, the most egregious of
all composers. He reminds you of what
Swinburne said about William Blake:
that, "aware that he must at least offend
a little, he did not fear to offend much.
To measure the exact space of safety, to
lay down the precise limits of offence,
was an office neither to his taste nor within
his power." Yet Strauss is irrefragably

the most commanding music-maker since Wagner—one of the great tone-poets. His capacities are difficult to bound. He has written pages that are among the greatest in all music. Such things as the love music in "Heldenleben," the tenth variation and finale in "Don Quixote," certain of the songs, the recognition scene in "Electra," the stupendous opening measures of "Zarathustra"—music of terrifying, of cosmic, sublimity: things such as this the world will not soon let die. We have mentioned Blake—of whom Strauss not infrequently reminds one; and it was Blake who finely and truly said that music "exults in immortal thoughts." There are immortal thoughts in the music of Strauss. At his best he is comparable only with the masters. He recalls that astonishing portrait of a famous publicist by John Sargent, which, if you cover one side of the face, suggests a diabolical creature without soul or conscience, whereas, if you cover the other

side, the face of an inspired and noble
dreamer emerges from the canvas. That
is Strauss: an amazing and inexplicable
compound of the great and the unworthy,
the trivial and the sublime, of virtue and
depravity—a grotesque and disturbing
phenomenon: a being half gamin and
half seer, a rogue as incorrigible as his
own "Till Owlglass," whose lips, though
they utter blasphemies, have yet been
touched with the sacred fire: a poet whose
eyes behold apocalyptic visions while his
hands play unspeakable pranks. The
world has never seen his like. He has
had no precursor. He is an anomaly—
unanticipated, incomparable.

He is not yet—he will not be for years
—justly valued. There are many who
will regard such praise as I have
written above as hyberbole of the most
unconscionable sort. The man has given
us a dozen masterpieces of the first rank;
yet for many he is still a mountebank,
a charlatan, a sensationalist, a pretentious

mediocrity without a single important claim to the esteem of his contemporaries.

Nothing could demonstrate this more pointedly than the fact that what is for some his undoubted masterpiece has sunk, during the brief period since it was put forth, into a condition that is almost neglect. It is barely six years since "Electra" was given to the world; and to-day it counts for almost nothing among any but the most devoted of Strauss's admirers. Yet I believe that this tremendous music-drama will some day take its place among the supreme things of music.

"Electra," at the time of its production, raised almost as dense a cloud of critical and journalistic dust as its immediate predecessor, "Salome." It would be profitless to rehearse the details of the controversy. A considerate providence—whose instrument one is happy to recognize upon this occasion as Richard

Strauss himself—had so ordered matters
in the first place that the debate, while
idly curious, idly sensational, and inevitably stupid, for the most part, did not
turn, as in the case of "Salome," upon
any question of ethics. For that let grate-
ful praise be rendered. Strauss, by his
choice of a dramatic subject, left no opening for the irruption into the discussion
of "Electra" of those frenetic champions
of æsthetic respectability whose capacity
for moral indignation is in inverse proportion to their capacity for lucid and in-
telligent analysis, and whose pursuit of
impudicity in art is as tireless as their
flair for it is acute. They who honestly
deprecated certain aspects of "Salome"
were compelled to summon heroic qualities of self-sacrifice and martyrdom; for
they had to see themselves ranged on the
side of a legion of clamorous defenders of
the public's moral health who had never
taken the trouble to read the play of
Wilde or hear the music of Strauss, and

116

whose ferocious objections were persistently directed against the wrong things. "Electra" provides no occasion for the activity either of moral policemen or of disquieted martyrs. It has no important sex element, either conventionally romantic or supposititiously illicit. Objection to the work has been centred, first, upon the alleged brutality, violence, and ignoble horror of its dramatic basis—the play of Hugo von Hofmannsthal; and, secondly, upon the alleged recklessness, extravagance, and general enormity of Strauss's score, its outrageous infraction of every established law of musical procedure. The latter charges are abundantly familiar in the case of Strauss; so let us consider now rather the characteristics of the drama upon which he has based his remarkable music.

Hugo von Hofmannsthal is young, a "modern," a "decadent"; and therein is the rock of his offending. One of the most acute of critics has written, in a rare and little-known book, these memorable sentences: "There is no inherent reason why a poet of to-day should not overtake the same themes as Æschylus overtook from Phrynicus, and Sophocles from Æschylus, and Euripides from all three. . . . The difficulty is not in the remoteness of the theme, still less in the essential substance. It is in the mistaken idea that the ancient formal method is inevitable, and in the mistaken idea that a theme sustained on essential and elemental things and therefore independent of unique circumstance can be exhausted by the flashing upon it of one great light. . . . Tradition says, if you would write of the slaying of Clytemnestra you must present a recognisable Electra and a recognisable Orestes; . . . but, to the spirit, Electra and Orestes are simply abstract terms of the theatre of the imagination . . . and the old Greek background is but a remembered semblance of a living stage that is not to-day what it was yesterday or shall be to-morrow, and yet is ever in essentials the same." It is doubtful if Herr von Hofmannsthal ever read those obscure and forgotten words; yet he might seek and find in them, if he cared to, a singularly anticipated justification for the impiety which has been charged against him—that of "modernizing" (as it has been called) Æschylus, Sophocles, and Euripides. He has been sternly reprehended because his Electra and Orestes are not "a recognisable Electra and a recognisable Orestes"; and the thrice-familiar epithets of contemporary denigration have been conferred upon him—his play is "lurid," "morbid," "neurotic"; and its lack of the "classic purity" of the Greek originals is missed and lamented. All of which is either untrue or beside the mark.

Von Hofmannsthal has chosen to construct a tragedy out of the ancient tale which inspired the "Electra" of Sophocles and Euripides and the middle play

of Æschylus's "Oresteia" trilogy, the
"Choëphoræ." He has gone for his plot
to the drama of Sophocles, the action of
which, in the main, he follows. As in
the play of Sophocles, Electra is the protagonist—Orestes is the mere instrument
of her purpose. Von Hofmannsthal has
italicised and intensified the theme
of her unquenchable grief, her consuming and invincible passion for retri-
bution. He has made her an extraordinary dramatic creation. As he conceives
her, she is incarnate hate, its very type
and image—a ragged, glaring, dis-
hevelled Mænad: a "wild cat," say the
servants, who screeches and snarls in her
execrations, and dwells among the dogs
in the courtyard; while to her mother she
is a "puff-adder." In her "poor, sad cor-
ner," says Electra, she lives, yet does not
live, feels nothing that women feel. She
has taken hatred for her bridegroom, and
only curses and despair have come forth
out of her body. Yet, tattered, degraded,

outcast as she is, there is nothing in the world, says one of the serving-women, so royal as she is—"she lies in rags upon the threshold, ay, but there is none in the house that can endure to look into her eyes."

It is in the conception of this vivid and truly appalling figure that the dramatist has fallen foul of his critics, many of whom appear to cherish the belief that her prototype, the Electra of Sophocles, was a very different sort of person. As a matter of fact, the heroine of Sophocles's play is by no means an altogether noble or exalted character. The Greek Electra tells of her "shrill-toned shrieks"; she demands "satisfaction with blood for blood"; the Chorus speaks of her as "breathing rage" in her interview with her mother; and at the moment when Orestes strikes down Clytemnestra we hear her, as we hear her descendant in the play of von Hofmannstahl, urge on her brother to "strike, if thou hast strength, a double stroke." The learned Buckley, in the introduction to his translation of Sophocles's play, speaks of Electra as "a virago almost bereft of female feelings"; he speaks of her "love that has been sharpened into keen hatred," of her "vindictive wrath," of her "accumulated bitterness," her mournings that teem with selfishness. Nor have other commentators a kinder word to say of her. She is a dreadful figure in Sophocles; she is a dreadful figure in von Hofmannsthal. It is wiser, in considering the play of the modern dramatist, to abstain from Pecksniffian comparisons, especially when these are based upon premises that are unsound. The just view will regard it apart from its classic prototypes, as a modern fantasy upon an antique theme, dealing with passions that are independent of any age or any country—with the universal and timeless stuff of tragedy.

Considered thus, von Hofmannsthal's

tragedy must be appraised as a remarkable and an impressive work. Its power is irresistible. It is steeped in the atmosphere of tragic horror, but this horror is wholly upon the plane of imaginative communication; there is nothing to shock the eye of the spectator; the catastrophe occurs, after the Greek fashion, off the stage. The suggestion of impending doom, of an inescapable, intangible, cumulative dread, is established and maintained with a surety and power which completely possess the mind. The play contains nothing so fearful to the sight or to the mind as the tableau at the close of Æschylus's "Choëphoræ," when Orestes is revealed standing over the body of his slain mother, with the horror of the thronging Furies growing in his eyes; nor has it anything to cause the horripilation which must have been felt by the Athenians at the shambles disclosed by the rolling back of the eccyclema at the conclusion of the "Agamemnon."

It is undeniable that the drama would be stronger, and that it would have an elevation which it now lacks, if von Hofmannsthal had put greater stress upon the Greek conception of vengeance as a religious duty—the idea which, more than anything else, exalts and ennobles their tragedy. It is true that Orestes, in the modern "Electra," has a speech in which he declares that he knows the gods have laid the deed upon his soul, and that they will spurn him if he shudders at it; but there is no such insistence upon this motive as we find in the Greek plays. Nor can it be denied that the play lacks simplicity and economy of diction, and that the models which have served in the elaboration of its details are at times obvious. There is a quality of speech, a certain use of symbolistic expression, that comes straight out of Maeterlinck; there is imagery which reminds us that the "Salome" of Oscar Wilde is highly appreciated in Germany and Austria. In the speeches of Clytemnestra, Electra, Chrysothemis, there is much rhetoric— some of it beautiful, poetical, strikingly eloquent; some of it artificial and over- sophisticated. Electra herself is at times as elliptical and enigmatic of speech as Hilda in Ibsen's "Master Builder." She is prone to ruminate elaborately and at length, when she should be direct and sparing of utterance and unhesitating in action. And there are times when she philosophises upon the nature of hate and love as mystically and superfluously as the transfigured daughter of Herodias in the final scene of the tragedy of Wilde. At such moments we are far indeed from both the spirit and the letter of Greek tragedy. But for all its derivations, arti- ficialities, and excrescences, the play has indisputable power, and at its finest it has beauty and imagination of a high order. It strikes the authentic note of tragic terror and tragic awe, and from it issues at times "the terrible whisper of destiny"; so that one recalls again the calm and tolerant words of him whose wisdom has before been adduced, and who knew that we may legitimately see Electra and Orestes, not as either Æschylus or Sophocles has revealed them to us, but as revealed to a vision that is of to-day, "shaped from the mould that moulds the spirit of to-day, and coloured with the colour of to-day's mind."

Æschylus's Cassandra, entering tremblingly the Palace of the Atridæ to meet the death which she knows is awaiting her there, cries out in terror that she detects an odour which reeks "like the breath of charnels." There is, in the "Electra" of von Hofmannsthal and Strauss, a similar exhalation for the imagination—an oppressive and unnamable menace in the air, a pervading atmosphere of terror, of unspeakable perturbation. This mood is implicit in the texture of the play; but it is marvellously enforced and intensified in the music of Strauss.

The music-drama was performed for the first time at the Dresden Royal Opera in January, 1909. It thus followed "Salome," its immediate predecessor, after an interval of three years. The first thing to be said is that "Electra" succeeds, where "Salome" failed, in being an almost continuously fitting expression of its subject-matter, von Hofmannsthal's drama. The nature of this subject-matter is of a character which taxes the expressional capacity of Strauss where it is strongest, and not, as in "Salome," where it is weakest. Strauss has, as a rule, been curiously ineffective in his treatment of the emotions of sex, and in "Salome" the music is least satisfying in the passages wherein the composer sought to delineate the desires of the uneasy protagonist of Wilde's play. But Strauss has a superlative gift for rendering, through the potency of tonal imagery, moods of terror, suspense,

127

awe, foreboding, ominous and sinister
gloom. He has a power of communicat-
ing the characteristic emotion of tragic
horror which continually reminds one of
Webster at his best. He is primarily a
musical tragedian, whose imagination is
most congenially and profitably employed
when it is dealing with the darker and
more dreadful stuff of tragedy.

"Electra" gives him precisely the kind
of subject which he is most fortunate in
depicting. Regarded simply as a tonal
italicisation of the action and emotions
of the play it is superbly successful. It
has a cyclonic sweep and power, a demo-
niacal intensity, which are well-nigh un-
bearable in their assault upon the nerves.
From the abrupt and sinister opening to
the wildly triumphant close the grip of
the music relaxes for scarcely a moment—
and when it does momentarily relax, it
is significant to observe, it is in the passages which Strauss has designed to de-

note the conjugal longings of Chrysothemis.

In its quality as sheer music the score
displays in a marked degree the strange
blending of strength and weakness, of
genius and futility, of inspiration and
paltriness, which are characteristic of
every phase of Strauss's intellectual activity. There are wonderful things in it—
passages which no one but Strauss would
have dared or accomplished. Of such are
the interview between Electra and her
mother, the passage in which the sisters
mourn the death of Orestes, the inimi-
tably ironic scene in which Electra lights
Ægisthus to his doom, and, above all, the
profoundly affecting recognition scene
between Electra and her brother: here
we have once more the deeper and finer
Strauss, the supremely moving and inspired tone-poet who portrayed the home-
coming and the death of Don Quixote,
who gave us the tranquil close of "Ein
Heldenleben." This scene is the musical

apogee of the work. It has a richness of emotion, a depth of sorrowful tenderness, which set it among the noblest things in music. But side by side with these memorable passages are others which are far from memorable—passages in which, as so often with Strauss, the music declines from power and vitality into a lamentable emptiness and commonness, and we get pages of the most arrant and undisguised commonplace; as, for example, in the music accompanying the lament of Chrysothemis over her single and childless state—music which is conspicuous for its melodic sentimentality and its trivial waltz rhythms—and in the famous dance of Electra which brings the work to an end in a veritable orgy of inflated banality.

Much might be said of the bland audacity, the superhuman ingenuity, the incredible mastery of technical resources, which have gone to the making of this astonishing score; but they are its least important aspects, and they have in the past been abundantly dwelt upon, gasped at, denounced, applauded. It is better to insist that this score is masterly in its dramatic truthfulness, the constancy with which the eye of the composer is fixed upon the object to be depicted. It is full of his typical qualities. Strauss displays here, as elsewhere, almost every defect except weakness; *that* he never has. He may exasperate by his commonness, his effrontery, his crudity, his inanity, his folly, or by his often unabashed sentimentality. But weakness—of that he cannot justly be accused; as it has been said of another, he has limitations, but no infirmities. He never halts or fumbles; he has a superb assurance. His mastery of his imaginative material and of his technic is absolute. He never fails to give one a sense of power. There is always, too, something of the cyclopean in Strauss. He startles us by the magnitude of his conceptions, the vastness of his designs, the huge sweep of his brush over the orchestral canvas. He may shock us by his crassness, or distress us by his silliness, or annoy us by his banality; but—and this is the essential point—he never loses his grip upon us. His magnetism is continually operative, even when (and the statement is not paradoxical) it repels.

IV

THE QUESTION OF OPERA IN ENGLISH

THE QUESTION OF OPERA IN ENGLISH

In writing not long ago upon that far too acrimoniously debated subject, Opera in English, Mr. Henry Edward Krehbiel genially recalled the broad smile which, in the lamented days of the National Opera Company's struggles with lyric drama in the vernacular, used to overspread the audience when the impersonator of Lohengrin, in the course of the scene before the cathedral, pealed forth in stentorian song the deeply impressive words, "Elsa! with whom conversest thou?" A quarter of a century has passed since that memorable and ill-starred attempt to establish here opera in the speech of the people; yet it was only a brief while ago that those who witnessed the production of Mr. Frederick

S. Converse's opera, "The Sacrifice,"
heard one of the characters sing this line
—a line enclosed by music of characteristically modern intensity: "Captain Burton, my dear aunt wishes to see you."
And who can forget that moment in
Colonel Savage's English version of
"Parsifal" a few years ago when the guile-
less hero repulsed the temptress in the
garden with, "Pernicious one! Get thee
from me!"

Now, it is undeniable that a prejudiced
opponent (if there be any such) of the
project of giving opera in the English
language might not ineffectively dispose
of the entire question by citing these
three examples of how opera in English
really works out in practice. The English-speaking Lohengrin whose words
amused the National Opera Company's
audiences was, beyond reasonable doubt,
employing the best available English
translation of Wagner's text; so was the
English-speaking Parsifal. The lady in

NATURE IN MUSIC

Mr. Converse's opera who bore a message from her aunt was speaking an original English text, devised by the composer himself for musical setting. Yet in each case that illusion of exalted speech which opera must maintain, if it does nothing else, was for a time rudely and utterly destroyed. For my own part, since I am anything but a prejudiced opponent of whatever ideals seem to make for æsthetic enlargement, I cheerfully grant that these instances are very far from proving the case against English opera: they simply show what it is capable of at its worst. Also they serve to point an essential distinction which should be made, but which seldom is made, by those who discuss this perennial question. They who talk of "opera in English" are apt to confuse two totally different things: operas written to original English texts, and operas sung with texts translated from the German or French or Italian into the vernacular. It is clear, of course, that we are dealing here with two separate matters; with ideals and ambitions that are by no means synonymous; with projects that differ widely in merit and in viability. It is one thing to long for and to promote operas written by American composers to English texts; it is quite another thing to long for and to promote the performance of operas by Wagner, Gounod, Puccini, with translated texts. Mr. Converse's "The Sacrifice" is one thing: a homogeneous product in which the music and the words (whatever their separate virtues) were made for each other; "Lohengrin" in English is a wholly different thing: an attempt to substitute for words that belong to Wagner's music, words that do not belong to it and that cannot be made to belong to it. There is bound to be futility in any discussion of "opera in English" which does not recognise that there are really these two distinct ideas included under the loosely applied title.

NATURE IN MUSIC

The plea that is most generally made for singing all foreign operas—whether German, Italian, Bohemian, French, or Russian—with texts translated into English, is that it is highly desirable that American audiences should understand the words that are sung by Siegmund and Romeo, Tosca and Mélisande, Turridu and the Queen of Spades: that inasmuch as operas, whether foreign or native, are as a rule sung in the vernacular when they are performed in Paris or Berlin or Milan, it is absurd and anomalous to ask a New Yorker to listen to "Aïda" or "Tristan und Isolde" or "Thaïs" sung in languages which he cannot understand; and that Opera can never be truly "educational" until it can be readily comprehended by the most ignorant.

Now there are so many fallacies, so many false premises, bound up in this indisputably plausible argument, that it is hard to disengage them all. The first thing that may be said in response to

those who long for the advent of what
may be called, for convenience, "Anglicised opera" (to distinguish it from English opera—that is, opera in which the
original text is in the vernacular) is that
its realisation is not a thing of the future,
but of the past. Every student of operatic
history in America knows, if he takes the
trouble to think back over the records,
that Anglicised opera is an old story in
this country. It has been tried again and
again, as it doubtless will be tried again
and again in the future. The American
Opera Company tried it at the Academy
of Music in 1886, and later tried it again
as the National Opera Company. Oscar
Hammerstein tried it at the old Manhat-
tan Opera House as early as 1893. The
redoubtable Colonel Savage tried it for
years in Boston, in New York, in "the
provinces," and we heard even "Meistersinger," "Parsifal," and "Walküre" in
Anglicised versions. And it is still being tried. The Century Opera Company

of New York is to-day giving meritorious second-rate performances of standard operas in the vernacular.

So it is not altogether easy to see why the champions of Anglicised opera should be cast down, or why they should go to the length of forming societies for the furtherance of their hopes. But they insist that they will not rest until it is no longer possible to hear in this country an opera sung in the language to which the music was written. If that is the way of musical salvation, well and good; but is it? Even the evangelists of the new faith admit that it has certain undesirable features, but they refuse to acknowledge the really grave objections that may be raised against it.

The most serious of these objections may be stated briefly thus: There is no such thing as a satisfactory operatic translation—and in using the epithet "satisfactory" I am exercising an exemplary moderation. Some are

less heinous than others; but most
translations of operatic texts, especially into English, are a source of genuine distress to anyone who is able to
understand the original. Music which is
written to express a particular set of
words cannot be made to express a quite
different set of words. In the first place,
the musical accent will, unavoidably, fall
time and again upon the wrong words or
the wrong syllables. Specific examples
will make this clear. Wagner, in
setting Venus's words near the close
of the first scene of "Tannhäuser,"
"Nicht halt' ich dir!" naturally
stressed the word *nicht,* setting it as a
high and sustained G. In Lady Macfar-
ren's translation (the standard one) this
line becomes, "I hold thee not!" with the
stress falling erroneously and absurdly on
the "I." Or turn to the seduction scene
in the second act of "Parsifal" and observe the grotesque misfit of Mr. Corder's English text, in comparison with

the concise and exquisite conformity of
Wagner's words and music, at Kundry's
phrase, *"Der Liebe ersten Kuss."* Of
course the last word is the essential word,
and Wagner has so treated it; but in Mr.
Corder's English version its equivalent,
"kiss," falls in an entirely different place
and is sung to a comparatively subordi-
nate note. Or, yet again, examine Mr.
Henry G. Chapman's English text (one
which is much above the average of its
kind) to "Pelléas et Mélisande." *"Vous
êtes un géant"* (Act I, Scene I) becomes,
"A giant's what you are," which is not
only feeble and foolish in itself, but is
completely at odds with Debussy's ac-
centing of the French words. Later
(Act III, Scene IV), *"A propos de la
lumière"* becomes, " 'Tis about the light
or something," with the musical stress
falling vapidly upon "or something" instead of upon *lumière*. Later still (Act
IV, Scene I), Mélisande's words, *"Je te
verrai toujours,"* become, "I shall al-

ways see you," with "see you" stressed instead of *toujours*. Examples could be multiplied indefinitely: there is scarcely a translated opera score that does not yield instance after instance of this sort of maladjustment.

In the second place, apart from the difficulty of devising a substitute set of words that will fit at every point the composer's scheme of musical accentuation, there is not only the formidable difficulty of preserving the actual sense of the original text, but the almost insuperable difficulty of preserving its connotations— its virtually untranslatable intimations of feeling and shades of fine significance. The English translators have naturally not been able to surmount these difficulties. Those who insist on listening to Wagner in English must be prepared to hear Wotan's *"Unverschämt und überbegehrlich macht euch Dumme mein Dank"* rendered as, "Shame devoid and shockingly covetous such conduct I call";

to hear the *"Treuloser Holder! Seligste Frau!"* of Isolde and her knight declaimed as "Faithless enfolder! Blissfulest bride!" In "Carmen" they will hear Micaela in her prayer sing, "I'll speak in her face of my duty," instead of *"Je parlerai haut devant elle"*; and Don José will say, " 'Tis she my heart is bent on," instead of *"Je la prendrai pour femme."* In "Tosca" they will hear Mario's passionate " . . . *Tanto la Vita!*" sobbed out as, "So dear; no, never!"

Such fatuities are present in all operatic translations, even the best; in most of them they are rife. A man would need to be a musician and a poet of inspiration and fabulous skill in order to achieve the task of providing, say, "Siegfried," with a viable English text, let alone one that would give satisfaction to an appreciative lover of the original. The adherents of Anglicised opera do not appear to realise that the musical setting of a text is indissolubly bound up with the particular

genius of the language employed by the
composer. Tristan's *"Ach, Isolde, wie
schön bist du!"* easily translatable though
it is, loses something definite and precious
as soon as one attempts to turn it into any
language save German. And one cannot
help pitying from the bottom of one's
heart the plight of the translator confronted with the reiterated *"petit père"*
of the child Yniold in "Pelléas et Mélisande"—"dearest father" is the best that
Mr. Chapman can do with it.

The question, then, naturally arises,
Why go to such pains to achieve so disappointing a result? Is it fair to the
composer? Is it conducive to a just ap-
preciation of masterworks? Is it in any
true sense "educational" to present a deli-
cately adjusted combination of words
and music in such a way that their relationship is distorted and their significance belied? Would it not be better
to encourage the hearer to acquire a

working knowledge of the few languages in which opera is usually sung in this country? Or he might resort to the simpler expedient of familiarising himself with a translation of the libretto in advance. The answer is made that what is good enough for the Germans and the French and the Italians should be good enough for us: that if Berlin can stand "Carmen" in German, we ought to be able to stand it in English. But surely it is Berlin's misfortune, not its happiness, that it cannot, as we can, hear "Carmen" sung in the language to which it was composed. There is no other country in the world where one can enjoy the inestimable privilege of hearing most of the operatic masterworks as their composers intended them to be heard—where in one theatre within one week it is possible to hear "Carmen" in French, "Tristan" in German, "Tosca" in Italian. Why, in the name of all that is enlightened, should we seek deliberately to impose upon ourselves the limitations of less fortunate peoples—to barter our unique advantage for the dubious privilege of hearing Micaela say, "I'll speak in her face of my duty"; of hearing Tristan addressed as "faithless enfolder"; of hearing, "So dear; no, never!" pealed to the strains of Mario's well-loved song of despairful reminiscence?

Let us now consider the much more agreeable subject of English opera— operas composed to original English texts. Here is a matter that invites a hopeful attitude on the part of the musical publicist. Of course there is not the slightest question that the production of operas by native composers set to texts in the vernacular is a highly desirable thing. No one who is interested in the growth of a native musical art but would rejoice to see operas by American composers, sung in the vernacular, established in the regular repertoire of, say, the Metropolitan Opera House. But obviously, of course, you must first catch your composer, not to speak of your librettist. The story of native opera-making in this country reaches back to the eighteenth century, but not many of those now living can remember anything anterior to George F. Bristow's "Rip Van Winkle," produced at the Academy of Music, New York, in 1855, and W. H. Fry's "Leonora," given at the same house three years later. But we can all recall Mr. Walter Damrosch's "Scarlet Letter," which he brought forward in 1896, and his later "Cyrano"; and the exhibition of Mr. Converse's "Pipe of Desire" and "The Sacrifice," of Mr. Herbert's "Natoma" and "Madeleine," of Professor Parker's "Mona," are matters of very recent history. In none of these works is there the breath of life. Either by reason of weak or amateurish librettos or dull, derivative, mediocre music, they have fallen short of the

149

standard which must be maintained if our native operatic art is to have anything more than a parochial interest and importance. It seems odd that it should need to be said, yet there are many who fail to perceive the glaringly evident and frequently stated truth that a poor opera is no better for having been composed by an American.

It is pleasant to hope, it is possible even to believe, that there are now living in this country composers capable of producing effective and distinguished lyric dramas. There is no lack of available texts. Certain plays by Mr. Yeats, by William Sharp, by Stephen Phillips, for example, are admirably suited to operatic treatment. The English language, heedfully and poetically employed, is a noble and an eloquent vehicle for musicodramatic speech. It is futile to attempt to make impressive operas with the kind of librettos used by Mr. Herbert in "Natoma" and Mr. Converse in "The Sacrifice." The artistic and memorable English opera will contain no verse of the quality of Mr. Redding's

> "Gentle maiden, tell me,
> Have I seen thee in my dreams,
>   I wonder?
> When above my pillow
> From the night fell starry gleams,
>   I wonder?"

nor such lines of dialogue as Mr. Converse's egregious "Captain Burton, my dear aunt wishes to see you." It will do no good for the composer who permits himself to accept such things to point an exculpatory finger at the preposterous librettos of certain operatic masterworks. "The Magic Flute" and "Trovatore" prevail, of course, despite their librettos, not because of them. It is absurd to suppose that the composer of today is justified in setting a weak or foolish libretto merely because Mozart and Verdi were indifferent or undiscriminating enough to be willing to do so. And, moreover, it is not easy to write music which, like theirs, can make us forget the poverty or silliness of its literary and dramatic subject-matter.

There is, besides, the question of securing singers of the first rank who can make themselves understood in English. Doubtless they can be trained to do it. The process will be difficult, but it is not impossible of accomplishment. When an opera in the vernacular can be entrusted to singers who will enunciate the English text with the lucidity and intelligence exercised upon French by, for example, the unforgettable Maurice Renaud, English opera will seem a less elusive dream than it does at present.

V

A NOTE ON MONTEMEZZI

A NOTE ON MONTEMEZZI

To an observer of the musical heavens
the discovery of a new composer is as
thrilling an event as the discovery of a
new star must be to those who watch the
more fruitful heavens of actuality. By "a
new composer" one means, of course, a
new composer of parts—one who speaks
with a voice that is arresting by reason
of its beauty, or its volume, or its distinction. To have lived in the day of, say,
Wagner's emergence must have been an
electrifying experience indeed—though
there is the hideous possibility that even
the most liberal, the most unimpeded,
among us might have reacted to him as
did Ruskin to "Die Meistersinger,"
which he dismissed, with delightful
vehemence, as an "affected, sapless, soulless, tuneless doggerel of sounds; . . . as

for the great *Lied,* I never made out
where it began or where it ended, except
by the fellow's coming off the horse-
block." But if we cannot all have been
present on that incomparable occasion,
there are many of us who have had the
scarcely less inestimable privilege of
watching the wonder and loveliness of
a "Pelléas" flush the tonal skies with
a beauty as magical and melancholy
as an autumn sunset, or have seen an
"Electra" flame in those selfsame skies
like the terrible burning star of the
Apocalypse, the name of which was
wormwood, and which embittered the
waters into which it fell—"and many
men died of the waters, because they were
made bitter": and there, perhaps, is the
fitting motto for what I am about to say.

How is one to know whether the
flaming star is a fact or an hallucination?
How, that is to say, are we to know
whether our new composer is worthy of
our liking or not? We fancy the candid

pessimist would tell us that we may know the authentic from the delusive by remembering the words of the Scriptural narrative that we have just quoted. Are the waters embittered by the burning star? If they are, then (says our candid pessimist) you may know that Genius has come upon the earth. Has any genius— has any genuinely creative composer— ever failed to embitter the waters? When Ruskin called the music of "Meistersinger" a "soulless, tuneless, doggerel of sounds" he merely echoed the opinion of most of the critics and many of the public of his time. We all remember how the most important music composed since the death of Wagner—the music of Debussy and Richard Strauss—was greeted by those who should have been the first to announce and extol it. So that it might almost be stated as a critical axiom that you may know a masterpiece by the bitterness it precipitates; and that a work

157

which is hailed upon its appearance as a masterpiece is—something quite different. The new work of an innovating genius will always taste bitter in the mouth to all save a few. If it does not— if its flavour delights the palate at once— let the heedful beware!

All of which is prefatory to a consideration of a new opera, by a new composer, which has made more noise in America than any lyric novelty of recent years. I refer to Italo Montemezzi's "L'Amore dei Tre Re," the production of which in New York was the occasion of general and indisputably sincere rejoicings—rejoicings which would have been a fit greeting, indeed, for a new "Tristan und Isolde," and which awoke, in the memories of some, ironic recollections of the quite different reception that marked the disclosure of "Pelléas et Mélisande" and "Electra."

Montemezzi is a wholly new apparition in the operatic field, so far as the world at large is concerned. He is young —in the early thirties; and his native Italy had seen the production of "L'Amore dei Tre Re" only a year before it was given in New York. Nor is the dramatist who has supplied the literary basis of his opera much better known outside of Italy. Sem Benelli is a contemporary Italian poet, whose name is often bracketed by his countrymen with that of Gabriele D'Annunzio; but few non-Latin readers are familiar with his work. His "L'Amore dei Tre Re" is a "tragic poem" in three acts. It is a play that might have been written for musical enlargement, so ideally suited is it to the purposes of the lyric stage. It is almost as spare, as free from accessory elements, as is Wagner's "Tristan."

Fiora, wife of Manfredo, is a young princess who has been wedded against her will to the son of the conqueror of her people. She loves Avito, and, in her husband's absence, gives herself to him.

The blind and aged Archibaldo, jealous of his son's honour, surprises her in the arms of her lover and strangles her. As she lies dead he smears her lips with poison, thinking to entrap her lover when he shall come to kiss her. But it is not Avito alone whom he entraps; Manfredo, too, kisses desperately the poisoned lips of Fiora; and Archibaldo, entering then, and thinking he has caught the lover, wraps his arms about the body of his dying son. It is a heart-shaking utterance of the sightless old king upon which the curtain closes:

"Ah! Manfredo! Manfredo! Anche tu, dunque,
Senza rimedio sei con me nell'ombra!"

It is said by those who best know Italian that Signor Benelli has accomplished in this play a dramatic poem of conspicuous excellence as literature. Upon that point I have no right to an opinion. But, quite aside from its literary quality, the play, as a drama for the lyric stage, is beyond question admirable. It is simple, sensuous, passionate. It has power and pathos.

Would that one could honestly avoid saying that it is worthy of a more gifted composer than Signor Montemezzi! Let it be admitted at once, with all heartiness, that Montemezzi is a musician who commands respect. He is a composer of evident scholarship, of indubitable feeling, of deep seriousness and sincerity. It is certain that he has been profoundly moved by the drama he has undertaken to set, and that he is quite single-minded in his endeavour to heighten and intensify it in his music. He is obviously not concerned about wooing the ears of the groundlings. He has given us a score in which, from beginning to end, there is not a measure that can justly be called meretricious; a score that makes no *ad captandum* appeal whatsoever. He has applied himself with undivided earnestness and devotion to the task of setting

forth his dramatic theme with all the en-
hancing power of which he is capable.
There is here no defect of intention, but
only a defect of capacity. If dramatic
music of the highest order could be
achieved without inspiration, then Montemezzi would have given us a masterwork to which we all, without exception,
could offer homage. But for my part,
I see no profit in judging a work of art
save by the criterion of the best. To extol
a new work because it is not so bad as
some, or because its composer is very
young and may do better, or because he
might have done worse, seems, to say the
least, beside the point. I have a stub-
born conviction that there is no such
thing as a second-rate masterpiece. The
supreme obligation of music is to be eloquent: if it is not eloquent, it has failed.

It has been intimated that Montemezzi
is entitled to some kind of credit because
he is different from Puccini. Now it is
certain that Signor Puccini has many

faults, and has committed many æsthetic indiscretions. His place is assuredly not with the high gods of music. But he *can* be eloquent; and he has unescapable individuality—the two indispensable virtues which Signor Montemezzi has not. Montemezzi's ideas lack distinction; but, what is worse, they lack character. His music is wanting in profile; it has no marked personality. It has feeling, it is rhetorically impressive; but of true imagination it has little. I should not think of denying that the scene in "L'Amore dei Tre Re" which arouses the greatest enthusiasm in its hearers—the love scene of the second act—is extremely effective and exciting; Montemezzi has written music for this scene which is an excellent imitation of the real thing—music which the incautious and the non-exigent would assuredly defend as eloquent beyond question. But it is not a difficult thing for the resourceful composer of to-day so to manipulate the marvellous expressional

resources that modern music has acquired
from the masters of the past that all but
the most wary are beguiled into thinking
that they are listening to the authentic
speech of inspiration. Plagiarism is not
implied, for plagiarism is unnecessary. A
commonplace melody, if it be large-
moulded and passionate in accent, and uttered in an ascending *crescendo* by the
wonderful myriad-voiced orchestra that
is now at the disposal of any accomplished craftsman, can suggest with extraordinary similitude the veritable
tongue of genius. But that is not what
I mean by eloquence in music. I mean
the kind of eloquence that stabs the spirit
like a flaming sword; that strikes the
mind with an instant conviction that an
immortal saying has been uttered; that
floods the heart with something that is
part exquisite ecstasy and part exquisite
pain; that opens to the inward eye, for a
brief moment, a vision of the heights
where eternal Loveliness dreams its eter-

nal dream, and makes us know that we
have seen

> "Beauty itself amid
> Beautiful things."

It is no pleasure to disparage so ear-
nest, so dignified, so scrupulous, so high-
minded a musician as Signor Montemezzi, especially as it is possible for the
most exacting to listen with true pleasure
to many pages of his opera, wherein is
to be found a persuasive expression of
feeling that is always sincere and deep.
But to say or to imply that he has produced a score which is worthy to be
named in the same breath with a work of
essential genius like "Pelléas et Mélisande," or like "Electra," or even like
"Der Rosenkavalier," is merely to darken
counsel.

When all is said, however, one is far
from being insensible to a certain pathos
that is implicit in this noble and sincere,
yet disappointing expression of the indis-

putable talent of this true artist—the
pathos that envelops all those who love
with passion beautiful things: who try to
speak, however haltingly, however brok-
enly, of those mysteries which, after all,
are beyond speech: who are dreamers of
dreams: who have seen, and cannot forget; yet who are not without consolation:
for they know that "there will come a
time when it shall be light, and man shall
awaken from his lofty dreams, and find
his dreams still there, and that nothing
has gone save his sleep."

VI

THE PLACE OF GRIEG

THE PLACE OF GRIEG

It is a singular fact, for which one need not pretend to account, that in musical criticism (the youngest, most unreasoned, and most unguided of the arts) one is seldom made aware that a distinction has been drawn between what Matthew Arnold liked to call the "real" and the "historic" estimates. Yet it is difficult to see how we can arrive at any just appraisal of music or of creative musicians unless this vital difference is held steadily before the mind. For example, it has been perfectly possible for modern critics, recognising only the historic estimate, blithely to rank the admirable Haydn as a major symphonist; yet imagine—one need not say Arnold, but any sensitive and responsible critic of letters —ranking, for example, Pope as a major poet! Arnold, it will be recalled, in defining what he means by the "historic estimate" of poetry, observes: "the course of development of a nation's language, thought and poetry, is profoundly interesting; and by regarding a poet's work as a stage in this course of development we may easily bring ourselves to make it of more importance as poetry than in itself it really is": that is, we may fall easily into the error of mistaking the historic significance of the "Chanson de Roland," or of the verse of Pope, or Dryden, for an essential significance which, as poetry, it does not possess. We may fall, through carelessness or indifference, into such an error; but we do not expect a deliberate and reasoned criticism of letters to exhibit carelessness or indifference: we do not expect it to fail of distinguishing between the artistic stature of Pope and Shelley, of Dryden and Keats. Yet how often does our musical criticism distinguish in its judgments between a purely

historic estimate and a real estimate of
Haydn, of much of Mozart, of the lesser
Beethoven? The reason, it may be said
again, is not germane to this discussion:
the fact alone is pertinent.

Of Edvard Grieg, the most widely and
excusably popular music-maker since
Mendelssohn, it would be easy to say that
it is not now possible, since he has been
dead so short a while, to form any historic
estimate which should be in the least con-
clusive. But the objection would not be a
valid one: Grieg's relation to the past
of musical art, to its development, to its
present condition—even to its auguries of
the future—is not in the least difficult
to perceive. But it is, I conceive, far
more interesting and rewarding to view
his art in itself; to attempt to arrive at
an estimate of its absolute, rather than
is historic, significance.

Let us consider first, as a convenient
point of approach, the claims which have
been made for him, and the faults which

have been charged against his art. The
most persistent, and the most absurd,
claim that has been advanced for him is
that he was pre-eminent as an exponent
of nationalism in music. It is a claim
which is as negligible as it is unsubstan-
tiated. We could still affor l to ignore
this aspect of his art even if it were not
true, as Mr. Henry T. Finck, in his in-
imitable survey of Grieg's career and
works, affirms, that instead of exclaiming
over his music: "How delightfully Norwegian!" we should say: "How delightfully Griegian!" That Grieg, an ardent
and uncompromising patriot, made much
of his artistic allegiance to Norwegian
soil is of little significance. As the
French critic, Ernest Closson, wrote,
"Grieg has so thoroughly identified himself with the musical spirit of his country that the rôles have become, as it were,
reversed. His personality—a personality
which in itself has nothing in common
with the music of the people—seems to

have become the prototype of this same music of the people; and the composers, his compatriots, imitate and copy him quite innocently in the belief that they are simply making use of local colour." It is not intended to dispose too summarily or cavalierly of a principle which to a very large number of intelligences is of deep import; but it remains an indisputable fact that "nationalism" in music has never constituted a valid claim to creative eminence. Who are those in musical art who have been conspicuous as exponents of nationalism? Not Bach, not Beethoven, not Schubert, not Schumann, not Wagner, not Brahms, not Tchaikovsky; rather they have been minor prophets like Dvorák and certain of the Russians—those Liszt-sprung "barbarians"—contemporaries of the Tchaikovsky at whom they sneered—whose music is far more eloquent of the salon and the academy than of the forests and steppes. Therefore, one may be permitted, with all possible deference, to leave the question of Grieg's Scandinavianism to specialists in the discovery and exploitation of æsthetic patriotism, where it will be sure of adequate discussion.

Claims have been made for Grieg, upon the purely artistic side, which have done his fame a very positive harm. He was called "the greatest of living composers, with the possible exception of Saint-Saëns"—an amazing exception! It was said at the time of his death that he had "created the latest harmonic atmosphere in music"; that he was "one of the most original geniuses in the musical world of the present or past"; that his songs, in melodic wealth, are surpassed only by Schubert's; that in "originality of harmony and modulation" he is surpassed only by Bach, Schubert, Chopin, Schumann, Wagner and Liszt; that in his orchestration he "ranks among the most fascinating." These claims have been deliberately and responsibly made, and they have been passionately defended; yet that they can have been seriously urged seems well-nigh incredible. As to the melodic wealth of his songs, do they surpass in this respect the songs of Schumann or of Franz? As to "the latest harmonic atmosphere in music," Grieg's harmony, in comparison with that of his contemporary, Claude Debussy, sounds as comfortably unventuresome as do the naïve metres of Herrick beside the strange rhythms and subtle assonances of Mr. Yeats. In "originality of harmony" does Grieg compare for a moment with those who were writing at the same time he was —with Vincent d'Indy, with Richard Strauss, with Charles Martin Loeffler? As for his "fascinating orchestration," where does it stand in comparison with the gorgeously imaginative scoring of Rimsky-Korsakoff, the superb instrumentation of Strauss, the exquisite orchestral mastery of Debussy and Loeffler?—magicians beside whom Grieg, for all the delicacy and charm of his scoring, seems like a tentative amateur. Does the music of the Norwegian tone-poet deserve, is it helped by, such ruthless, wholesale, and inconsiderate praise?

On the other hand, let us see what certain of his detractors have found to urge against his art. The disapproval of his critics has been most pithily summed up, perhaps, by Mr. Daniel Gregory Mason, who reproaches Grieg because, he holds, he "is never large or heroic"; because "he never wears the buskin." "He has neither the depth of passion nor the intellectual grasp needed to make music in the grand style." Probably of all his peculiarities, complains Mr. Mason, "the most significant is the shortness of his phrases and his manner of repeating them almost literally, displaced a little in pitch, but not otherwise altered. . . . His thoughts complete themselves quickly; they have little span, and they are combined, not by interfusion, but by juxtaposition. He never weaves a tapestry; he assembles a mosaic." Intricacy of design, largeness of span, synthetic power, are qualities to be recognised and applauded; but are they essential to a masterpiece? Have they, finally, anything to do with the matter? What innate superiority, *per se,* has "a broad-spanned arch of melody," a phrase of large sweep and wide scope, over a "short-breathed" phrase? Consider, for instance, that extremely familiar masterpiece-in-little, the dirge, "Aase's Tod," from the first "Peer Gynt" suite. "Short-breathed" in structure it undeniably is, wholly naïve in its contrivance; yet is it any less deeply and largely tragic, less fine and memorable, less admirable a masterpiece, for being so? What, in the end, have expanse and magnitude, intricacy and elaborateness of plan, to do with the case? Is it true, as a somewhat impatient appraiser of Grieg has lately affirmed, that artists who have carried their inspiration "through a long and arduous process of eloquent exposition" are necessarily to be more greatly honoured than those who have completed their inspiration within a briefer flight? The contention has, beyond doubt, a deceptive force: a great epic seems, at first glance, obviously superior to a great lyric. There is Schubert's "Erlkönig," a superb song, of long flight, of broad scope; there is his "Der Tod und das Mädchen," also a superb song; but it is very short: it is only forty-three measures long, while the "Erlkönig" is one hundred and forty-eight measures long. Moreover, "Der Tod und das Mädchen" is utterly simple in structure, while the "Erlkönig" is varied in structure and rich in contrast. Or, take another instance: The E-major Intermezzo, opus 116 (No. 2), and the Third Symphony of Brahms are both authentic masterpieces; the first is among the most perfect of modern piano works in the smaller forms,

the second is one of the noblest of
modern symphonies; in quality of inspiration there is nothing to choose between
them. Is the symphony, then, by reason
of superior bulk, a more eminent masterpiece? "There is no perfect lyric," Mr.
Arthur Symons has finely and truly said
—and the sentence is an answer to the
question which has just been asked—
"there is no perfect lyric which is made
less great by the greatness of even a perfect drama."

May we not conclude that the
truth of the matter, as we must apply
it in Grieg's case, is that it is not *dura-
tion* of inspiration, but *quality* of inspiration, which counts, and which some-
how must be determined and appraised.
Is Grieg's accent the accent of great music, of music of the first class; has it the
accent, not necessarily of the few supreme
masters, but of authentic inspiration?
Has it any of the essential characteristics
of the best music? One may, not too

dogmatically, say that these essential characteristics are: ideas, individuality, imagination—I say nothing of "beauty," for that way lie inescapable pitfalls. By "ideas" one means definite and specific musical conceptions which persuade at once by their saliency, their eloquence, their distinction; and these concepts may be melodic, harmonic or rhythmic. "Individuality" and "imagination" are, of course, self-explanatory terms. To attempt to test all music by an application of these three touchstones would probably lead one, before long, into a critical quagmire; but they are of excellent service for purposes of rough classification. Let us say, for example, that in the music of Tchaikovsky we find extreme richness and fervour of imagination, vivid individuality, but not an abundance of distinguished or noble ideas; that in the music of his brilliant countryman, Rimsky-Korsakoff, we find extraordinary and audacious imagination, but little individ-

uality and few ideas; that in the music
of Saint-Saëns we find neither imagination, important and memorable ideas, nor
vital and persuasive individuality (his
technical expertness, his admirable crafts-
manship, is a virtue which one takes for
granted in a modern musician); that, to
pass to the other extreme, we find, in
the music of such men as Wagner and
Beethoven, superlative ideas, puissant individuality, and boundless imagination.
Now where, in this category, does Grieg
belong? With the men whose supreme
distinction lies in the transcendent quality
of their ideas? or with the men of restless and flaming, or exquisite, imagination? or with the men whose individuality is indubitable, but who lack salient
and original ideas and richness of imagination—men of the stamp of Mendelssohn, Massenet, Puccini, Goldmark?

Let us say that Grieg possesses, in a
measure, all of these excellences; but he
possesses them in an unequal degree. He

is sometimes truly imaginative, as in passages in the "Peer Gynt" music, in the last two sonatas for violin and piano (opus 13 and opus 45), in certain of the songs and piano pieces. He has, too, achieved ideas: ideas of exquisite distinction, of noble breadth. But they lack the stamp of supreme excellence; to resort to a literary analogy, his inspiration never attains to the kind of utter and perfect felicity which is represented, in poetic art, by such lines as these:

> "The sunrise blooms and withers on the hill
> Like any hillflower; and the noblest troth
> Dies here to dust."

There is music—music by Wagner, by Brahms, by Debussy—which is as beautiful, as supremely felicitous, as these lines; but Grieg does not command it. He is often captivating and delicious, eloquent and impassioned—as in many of his lovely songs; there is free and vigorous spontaneity, an infectious vitality, in the violin sonatas; in the dirge from the "Peer Gynt" suite the music has a quality of sadness and beauty which none save Grieg could have given it. To praise such things as these is as necessary as it is delightful. Yet it would be over-generous to say that they belong among the class of the very best, delectable and striking as they are.

But, in a surpassing degree, Grieg has individuality—individuality that is seizing and indubitable. That, one feels, is his distinguishing possession. His accent is unmistakable. His speech may sway one, or it may not; but always the voice is the voice of Grieg. You recognise it at once; there is no mistaking it. He has, beyond denial, his own distinguishing way of saying things, his own idioms—his own mannerisms, if you will. You hear a phrase from one of the lesser known sonatas for violin and piano, and you exclaim at once: "Grieg!" For the music is as redolent of him, and of none other, as

"O cloud-pale eyelids, dream-dimmed eyes. . ."

is redolent of Mr. Yeats, or as the recorded vision:

"Fair as in the flesh she swims to me on tears"

is redolent of Mr. Meredith. The music of Grieg, when he is at his best, is drenched in personality, in individual colour. It is curiously his own, curiously free from the reflection of other minds and other temperaments. In its earlier condition it reminds one at times of Chopin, of Schumann, of Mendelssohn, occasionally of Wagner; in its later stages it suggests no one but Grieg himself. Then, at such times, it is a rare voice that speaks, a voice of penetrating sweetness, a tender and vibrant voice, a voice of incomparable freshness and limpidity—no music-maker since Schubert has uttered tones so liquid and free, so spontaneous, unwearied and unworn. There have been others who spoke more entrancingly, more profoundly, more nobly, more subtly, with more importunate and commanding beauty; there are to-day, among those who but a short while ago were Grieg's contemporaries, music-makers who surpass this delectable lyrist in scope and vigour of imagination and fineness of thought. Yet Grieg is thrice-admirable in this: he wears no one's mantle; he borrows no man's speech.

VII

A MUSICAL COSMOPOLITE

A MUSICAL COSMOPOLITE

It is probably not realised by most music-lovers that, of the four or five living composers whose productions are indisputably important, one is a resident of the United States—a circumstance, it will perhaps be conceded, of more consequence to the future of musical art in this country than the fact that the composer who is meant was born, not in America, but in Alsace.

The ordinary composer, the composer as a type, is avid of publicity. It is the breath of his nostrils: without it, advancement, prosperity, success, are to him well-nigh inconceivable. He would dismiss as meaningless and absurd the lines of the poets of "Vagabondia":

"Success is in the silences,
Though fame be in the song."

189

NATURE IN MUSIC

Charles Martin Loeffler is a composer who is egregiously false to type. His indifference to publicity, to the promotion of his reputation, is extravagant. Whether his music be known or unknown, liked or misliked, praised or disparaged, is, to him, apparently a matter of very little moment. He has been slow to complete, reluctant to give forth. The earliest of the pieces which he has seen fit to retain in the list of his works date back almost a quarter of a century; yet there are to-day less than half a hundred compositions which he cares to acknowledge; he has discarded almost as much as he has retained. And, as I have said, he has been loath to yield his manuscripts to the engraver. Of the forty-odd separate compositions which to-day represent his avowed production only one-half have as yet been published.

Thus it is almost in despite of himself that Loeffler has achieved the celebrity that is his. It is celebrity of an enviable kind, for he is known chiefly among those who relish the finest and rarest that is done or attempted in the musical art of our time. In other words, he is most truly valued by epicures and connoisseurs; and that, assuredly, is a desirable and fortunate relation to bear to one's contemporary public.

Loeffler, though he was born at Mühlhausen, Alsace, in 1861, has lived and laboured in America for a generation as composer and violinist. His training as a music-maker was cosmopolitan; he studied his art in Berlin and in Paris, but his temperamental and intellectual sympathies have drawn him persistently toward France. Indeed, he might at one period of his career have been taken by the casual observer for a Frenchman *pur sang*. Almost all of the music which he composed between the years 1895 and 1901 was suggested by French texts; and in his "Quatre Mélodies," one of the works of that period, even the dedications are in French. His prepossessions are to-day less inalienably Gallic; but he still remains essentially a cosmopolite, though I believe he has been for some time a naturalised citizen of the United States.

Not long after he came to America, as a youth just entering his twenties, he joined the Boston Symphony Orchestra as one of the violins, and he served for many years as second concert-master in that illustrious organization. He retired from the orchestra in 1903; and now, on his farm near Medfield, Massachusetts, devotes himself for the most part to composition.

His works include orchestral and choral pieces, chamber music and songs. Though his knowledge of the resources of the piano is comprehensive, and though he writes for it with extraordinary skill in conjunction with the voice and with other instruments, he has contributed nothing to its solo répertoire. For orchestra he has composed four tone-poems: "La Mort de Tintagiles" (after Maeterlinck), "La Bonne Chanson" (after Verlaine), "La Villanelle du Diable" (after Maurice Rollinat), and "A Pagan Poem" (after Virgil). His chamber music includes a quintet in one movement for three violins, viola and 'cello; an octet for two violins, viola, 'cello, double bass, two clarinets and harp; two rhapsodies for oboe, viola and piano; and a sextet in one movement for two violins, two violas, two 'cellos, entitled "Le Passeur d'Eau." His songs comprise "Quatre Poëmes," for voice, viola and piano: "La Cloche Fêlée" (Baudelaire), "Dansons la Gigue!" "Le son du cor s'afflige vers les bois," "Sérénade" (Verlaine); "Quatre Mélodies": "Timbres Oubliés," "Adieu pour Jamais," "Les Soirs d'Automne," "Les Paons" (all to words by Gustave Kahn); "Four Poems": "Sudden Light" (Rossetti), "Sonnet" (George Cabot Lodge), "A Dream within a Dream," "To Helen"

(Poe) ; "The Wind among the Reeds":
"The Hosting of the Sidhe," "The Host
of the Air" (both to words by W. B.
Yeats) ; "Le Flambeau Vivant" (Baudelaire) ; "Vereinsamt" (Nietzsche) ; "Der
Kehraus" (Eichendorf) ; "Ton Souvenir
est comme un livre bien aimé" (Albert
Samain) ; and settings, as yet untitled, of
two poems from Vol. I of Gustave
Kahn's "Poésies." "By the Rivers of
Babylon" is a setting of portions of the
126th and 137th Psalms for women's
chorus, organ, harp, two flutes and 'cello;
"L'Archet," text by Cros, is a ballad for
mezzo-soprano, female chorus, piano and
viola; there is an eight-part chorus for
mixed voices *a cappella,* "For One Who
Fell in Battle," to words by T. W. Par-
sons; there is a setting of "The Ser-
mon on the Mount" for chorus, organ
and strings; and a one-act opera, based
upon a play by William Sharp, is in
process of completion. In addition to
these, there are a number of works of

early date which do not now satisfy the
composer and which he does not intend to
publish. Among these are a string quar-
tet in A minor, a "Divertimento" in the
same key for violin and orchestra, a "Fantastic Concerto" for 'cello and orchestra,
a suite, "Les Veillées de l'Ukraine" (after
Gogol), for orchestra and violin, a "Di-
vertissement Espagnol" for orchestra and
saxophone, a "Ballade Carnavalesque"
for piano, flute, oboe, saxophone and bas-
soon, a setting for voice and piano of
Baudelaire's "Harmonie du Soir," and a
string sextet in three movements, the middle one of which, revised, is the "Passeur d'Eau" referred to above.*

* Although virtually all of these works have been
performed, only one-half of them, as I have already
observed, have been committed by their meticulous
author to the printed page. In 1903 the "Quatre
Mélodies" were published as opus 10. The
"Quatre Poëmes" (opus 5) followed in 1904. To
the following year belong the rhapsodies for oboe,
viola, and piano (without opus number), "La Mort
de Tintagiles" (opus 6), and "La Villanelle du

Loeffler's artistic *terrain* is not easily
defined with exactitude. The literary in-
clinations of a modern composer are
usually a trustworthy guide to his temperament, to the colour of his thought,
to his *principia*. But Loeffler's tastes
range over a somewhat perplexingly wide
and diversified territory. He has been
moved to musical utterance by Poe and
by Virgil, by Maeterlinck and by Nietzsche; he apprehends Baudelaire, Rollinat, Rossetti, Verlaine; he is an inquisitive delver in the literature and philos-
ophy of alien peoples and forgotten civil-
isations; his intellectual curiosity is in-
satiable. Yet, on the whole, he has been
most strongly disposed toward the liter-

Diable" (opus 9). The "Four Poems" (opus 15)
were issued in 1906, "By the Rivers of Babylon"
(opus 3) in 1907, "The Wind Among the Reeds"
(without opus number) in 1908, "A Pagan Poem"
(opus 14) in 1909, and "For One who Fell in
Battle" in 1911. That, up to the present time, is
the whole of his published output.

ary *révoltés,* the mystics and visionaries,
of our own time; he has manifested a
natural kinship of thought and feeling
with Verlaine, with Baudelaire, with
Rollinat, with Gustave Kahn, with Maeterlinck, with Poe. He is far from being
a mere recrudescent Romanticist. He
has a love for the *macabre,* the fantastically sinister and tragical; but he in-
dulges it in a manner wholly free from
the excess and the attitudinising that are
an unmistakable index of the survival of
the Romanticistic impulse. His sincerity
and his instinct for proportion are con-
stant and unfailing. He can set to music
the poignant and terrible "Cloche
Fêlée" of Baudelaire, and the music is a
perfect reflex of the poem; yet it is impossible not to feel that it was written
by one whose soul is very different from
the soul of Baudelaire as exposed to us
by Mr. James Huneker: a soul "patient-
ly built up as a fabulous bird might build
its nest—cascades of black stars, rags,

leaves, rotten wood, corroding dreams, a spray of roses, arabesques of incense and verdigris. . . ." Even when Loeffler is most eloquently sinister, most disquietingly baleful, a rare tact, an unerring sense of measure and balance, a prophylactic humour, save him from extravagance and turgidity. His music permits us to ascribe to him a soul which could approximate the soul of Baudelaire at only a few points. He is capable of making us dream of black stars, and at times there is gall and wormwood in his music; but there is no decay and no squalor in it. With all his passion for the bizarre and the umbrageous and the grotesque, we are never in doubt as to the essential dignity, the essential purity and nobility, of his spirit: he is one of the *âmes bien nées*.

Au fond he is a mystic, a dreamer, a visionary. A mystic: for Loeffler has the mystic's bias toward that which transcends the immediate and the tangible phases of experience, the mystic's serene conviction of the reality of the extra-sensational. His imagination ranges most freely and familiarly in that psychic borderland where the emotions become indescribably rarefied and subtly heightened—where they become more the echo and reverberation of emotions than emotions themselves, yet gain rather than lose in intensity by the process. He is of the order of mystics whose thought, while it has the penetrative power of all mystical thought, is saturated with a quality of feeling that springs from an exquisite and supersensitive intuition of the human heart, rather than from sustained spiritual aspiration. That is to say, he is akin to Rossetti and Yeats and Maeterlinck rather than to Crashaw and Blake and Wordsworth.

Necessarily, therefore, he is both a visionary and a dreamer—a visionary whose thought is predominantly sombre and tragical; a dreamer oppressed by

NATURE IN MUSIC

"... the burden of the mystery ...
Of all this unintelligible world."

His most characteristic music is that to
which he has been moved by the imaginings of Verlaine, Rollinat, Poe, Maeterlinck, Baudelaire, in their autumnal
moods, their disconsolate hours. He has
seemed to be most congenially employed,
as he has been most persistently engaged,
in giving musical voice to thoughts of
which he is reminded by the darker
brooding of these masters of sorrowful
speech. He is shaken by the unutterable
sadness of human life, by the thought of
"the great stream of human tears falling
always through the shadows of the
world": the *lacrymæ rerum* obsess his
imagination, and he speaks his dolour
again and again, in accents that are by
turns mournful, anguished, despairing,
and resigned. His music is touched at
its core with an ineffable melancholy. It

is most typical when it issues from his imagination in slow

> "... swallow-flights of song that dip
>   Their wings in tears. ..."

He is at ease, not in Zion, but in the company of those who, grief-haunted and disillusioned, face the human pageant with the despair that cloaks itself in irony and bitterness. He is giving the truest account of his temperament when he is translating into music some of the more grievous and sinister imaginings of Rollinat, or some poem by Verlaine or Baudelaire filled with brooding menace and immitigable grief; or in his symphonic poem suggested by that most piteous and terrible of Maeterlinck's plays, "La Mort de Tintagiles"; or, as in one of his latest songs, when he is setting wild and *macabre* verses by Eichendorf.

It is true that he has responded to other emotional states. He has derived an orchestral song of rapturous lyric sweetness from the aubade which Verlaine addressed to his betrothed. The music that he wrote for Poe's "To Helen" is of a loveliness that might well fit it to serve as an apostrophe in illustration of the matchless lines of Wordsworth:

> " . . . and beauty born of murmuring sound
> Shall pass into her face."

His magnificent "Pagan Poem," provoked by the amorous incantation of the sorceress in Virgil's eighth eclogue, is largely and nobly rhapsodic. His *a cappella* chorus, "For One Who Fell in Battle," exhales a spirit of grief that is all transfiguring and uplifted tenderness rather than piercing and inconsolable regret. Latterly he dwelt for a time in Ildathach, the Many-coloured Land of the Celtic imagination, bringing forth some music—haunting, fantastic, of insinuating charm—derived from poems by the Irishman Yeats. He has, too, repeatedly given evidence of the fact that the ritual of the Church has exerted a powerful effect upon his imagination. But he returns ever and again to the contemplation of those darker moods of the soul which seem chiefly to stimulate his inspiration, and which compel his distinguishing performances as a music-maker. It is beyond dispute that the general aspect of his art is not eupeptic. He makes us feel as if he had consecrated himself to what Goethe called "the worship of sorrow"; or we seem to hear him repeating the plaint of Sir Thomas Browne that "the whole creation is a mystery . . . a dream or mock show, and we all therein but pantaloons and antics"; or we think of Leopardi and his insistence upon the *indegno mistero delle cose;* and at times we hear the very voice of Senancour: "Sensibility which no words can express, charm and torment of our vain years! vast consciousness of a nature everywhere greater than we are, and everywhere impenetrable!" He sounds this note again and again. It recurs insistently, a sombre undertone in his music, like the Dies Iræ whose characteristic progressions he introduces so often into the thematic structure of his pieces.

"Nothing is lost that's wrought with tears," said Blake; and since every personal revelation of life through art, so long as it be authentic and communicative, is infinitely precious, there can be no question of the value of such disclosures of temperament and experience as we get from Loeffler at his most typical. Certainly nothing could exceed the sincerity and the affecting eloquence of his art in whatever aspect he chooses to exhibit it; and he is never more sincere or more eloquent than when he gives sorrowful and responsive heed to

"Earth's old and weary cry."

Of the beauty and the importance of his music, *quâ* music, there will, in time, be no denial worth considering. After a quarter-century of curiously deliberate activity, of quiet devotion to what would have seemed to many an impossible ideal of perfection, he is at last coming into his own. He is recognised, among those whose sense of the best is surest, as one of that small group of living composers, to whom I referred at the start, whose deliverances are of prime artistic consequence. He shares with Strauss, with Debussy, with d'Indy, the distinction of pre-eminence over the lesser and varyingly admirable body of contemporary music-makers.

His artistic growth has been marked by eclecticism. His cosmopolitan training, his long years of orchestral service as an executant of other men's ideas, and an inexhaustible curiosity in all æsthetic and intellectual matters, have had their natural influence upon his music. He has absorbed a dozen musical temperaments, has known and betrayed their influence, has exhausted their power of stimulus, and has forgotten them; his own individuality has survived. It is possible to discern in his earlier work the impression made upon his sensitive psychic retina by Bach, by Wagner, by Berlioz, by Liszt, by Brahms; but he has finally wrought a style that is unmistakable and his own. There are pregnant moments, remarkable and original beauties, in his earlier work; but his speech has been wholly personal only in the music which he has produced within the last fifteen years. His "Quatre Poëmes," which were composed a decade and a half ago,—though they were not published until 1904,—expose clearly his typical traits. His harmonic and melodic style, the full flavour of his personality, may here be savoured for the first time. He has written nothing more completely characteristic than the second and third pages of "La Cloche Fêlée," the third and eighth pages of the "Sérénade" (the setting of the line, "Et ta douceur à me martyriser" is incomparable), the opening page of "Le son du Cor," and, in Dansons la Gigue!" the setting of

> "Je me souviens, je me souviens,
> Des heures et des entretiens,
> Et c'est le meilleur de mes biens."

It will be perceived by any receptive observer who examines or hears these songs that this is music quite solitary and apart, music which says new things in a peculiarly distinguished way.

His harmony is irrubrical, and it is highly individualised. It does not manifest Strauss's incorrigible audacity of procedure, his Olympian disdain of euphony; and in comparison with the obliquities of such nefast revolutionaries as Schönberg, Stravinsky, *et al.,* it seems almost old-fashioned. It is less fluid and prismatic than Debussy's, a good deal less acrid than d'Indy's. He uses freely effects derived from the eccle-

siastical modes, though their influence
upon him has not been so profound and
continuous as it has been upon Debussy.
His harmonic method is clearly the
product of an exceptional feeling for rich
and subtle combinations of tone, balanced
by an instinctive reticence, a sense of
form and balance, for which "classic" is
the just word. And the note of his style
as a harmonist is unmistakable. Such
passages as his setting of "Et ta douceur
à me martyriser," in the "Sérénade" (to
which I have already referred), the last
page of "Les Paons," the final measures
of "To Helen," the first six measures,
and the last page, of the "Sonnet," and
those portions of "La Mort de Tintagiles" in which the viola d'amore partici-
pates, could have come from no other
hand but Loeffler's.

I have instanced these passages chiefly
because of the striking and individual
quality of the harmonic idea underlying
them. But, notable harmonist though he

is, as a melodist Loeffler is still more remarkable. I am aware of no living melodist who combines, in equal measure, these qualities: on the positive side, originality of conception, an incorruptible fineness of taste, and the mastery of a style at once broad and subtle, passionate and restrained; on the negative side, a spontaneous avoidance of sentimentalism, triviality, and commonplace. They are not possessed in like degree by any one of his contemporaries. Strauss's frequent commonness, d'Indy's limited emotional compass, Fauré's slightness of substance, Reger's aridity, rank them, as melodists, definitely below Loeffler; while Saint-Saëns and Sibelius, Dukas and Ravel and Schönberg, Elgar and Rachmaninoff and Scriabine, are his inferiors at almost every point. As for Debussy, he is indeed an exquisite melodist, a creator of melodic thoughts that are incomparably lovely and of an unexampled rarity— thoughts that are as "dreams of the wavering images of dreams."

But Debussy has not Loeffler's blend of subtlety and power, of largeness and intensity. He has written nothing so broad and fervent, so passionate and full-throated, as the superb theme in A flat which is heard from the violins in the *poco piu mosso* section near the beginning of the "Pagan Poem"; or the equally superb melody in A minor, sung by the 'cellos and violas against *arpeggios* for the piano, which follows the first distant call of the trumpets behind the scene. In fact, the whole of this extraordinary score is pressed down and overflowing with melodic ideas of enthralling eloquence and beauty—melodically considered, it is a masterwork of the first order. Examine also (to adduce at random) his song, "Les Paons." I know of few more ravishing examples of pure lyric inspiration than the setting which he has given to the words,

NATURE IN MUSIC

"Nuit claire aux ramures d'accords,
Et la lassitude a bercé son corps
Au rythme odorant des pures musiques."

Consider, again, the song, "To Helen," which is a continuous fabric of melodic inspiration (how inevitable and how splendid is the expression which the composer has found for "the glory that was Greece and the grandeur that was Rome"!). These are typical, not isolated, instances of his melodic power. As with his harmonic style, his melody is unmistakable in its accent. It is impossible to think of the passages which I have cited as issuing from any brain but Loeffler's; or to ascribe to any other writer of music, living or dead, such equally typical things as the phrase marked "espressivo" in the piano part of "La Cloche Fêlée" just before the words "Qui, malgré sa vieillesse"; or the exceedingly characteristic melody in A major for the piano on the third page of "Adieu pour Jamais";

or the haunting phrase in triplets (*andante,* 12-8) which begins the second page of "La Cornemuse"; or the woful melody which opens "Le son du Cor"; or the chief themes of "La Mort de Tintagiles." If these are not the product of an inventive and imaginative capacity of the first order, it is puzzling to know what the signs of that capacity may be.

His individual employment of harmony, his excelling gift as a melodist, are supported by a technic that is secure and resourceful, and, in its mature development, masterful. He controls his medium with ease, whether he is writing for piano, for the voice, or for orchestra. He is a daring and felicitous contrapuntalist, a fertile contriver of rhythms; and as a painter upon the orchestral canvas he has a manner and a power that are his alone. He does not score with the witchery of the necromantic Debussy, nor with the overwhelming weight and plangency of Strauss; but he

has discovered hues and perspectives that
are unknown to them. He employs a
palette that can yield the barbaric splen-
dours of the "Pagan Poem," the pure
radiance of the morning-song after Verlaine, the sombre shadows that enwrap
the tragedy of Tintagiles and the Dread
Queen.

Always, in every exercise of his art,
he displays a fineness, a scrupulousness,
an exigent passion for perfection, that are
unparalleled in the musical art of to-day.
He has a more thoroughgoing detesta-
tion of the facile, the obvious, the inex-
pensive, than even the fastidious Debussy—I think he would be incapable of
certain Massenet-like sentimentalities to
which that singular genius seems to be
prone now and again. It is not easy to
imagine music more utterly free from the
note of platitude and Philistinism, or
from deliberate concessions of any sort,
than the music of Loeffler. He never employs those convenient æsthetic moulds

which, as Henry James has said, "condemn us to an eternal repetition of a few familiar *clichés."* His ideas are as fresh and unformularised as they are fine and sincere.

I have named Debussy in the course of certain contrasts and comparisons. A good deal has been made, by critics who are either undiscerning or incompetent, of an alleged indebtedness to Debussy on the part of Loeffler. It is true that Loeffler's music has certain external traits which it shares with the music of Debussy, of d'Indy, of Fauré, and of other musicians native to the country with which, in a spiritual sense, Loeffler is allied. These men use in common various harmonic and melodic expedients which, superficially, relate them, but which no more indicate an essential kinship than did, for example, the use of certain chromatic progressions by Liszt and Wagner indicate the interdependence of those two masters—Wagner's obvious and unashamed thematic borrowings from his long-suffering friend are another matter. The important fact, in the case of Loeffler and Debussy, is that their habit of thought and their manner of utterance are fundamentally different. Their natures impinge at a few points; they are both dreamers, both visionaries, and they both have the mystical temper; but in their intellectual outlook, in their spiritual and emotional preoccupations, they differ *toto cælo*. It is as impossible to think of Debussy as the composer of "La Mort de Tintagiles," the "Pagan Poem," "La Clothe Fêlée," or "To Helen," as it is to think of Loeffler as the composer of "Poissons d'Or," or "Nuages," or "Sirènes," or "L'Après-midi d'un Faune." Their temperaments and their styles are irreconcilable. It is this elementary and indisputable fact which makes the suggestion of an obligation on Loeffler's part unworthy and inconsiderable.

NATURE IN MUSIC

In the case of so complex, various, and restless a spirit as Loeffler's—one which is fed by many obscure and mysterious streams of consciousness—all generalisations should be tentatively held and advanced. I think, though, that I may say of him that his distinguishing characteristic, certainly his distinguishing achievement, is his consummate mastery of sorrowful speech. His creative gift flowers most perfectly when he is voicing moods of grief and lamentation. I think that he is then not only most truly and movingly himself, but that in this—in his power of expressing a peculiar and distinctive quality of sadness: a sadness burdened with wondering despair and haunted by a sense of mystery and terror—he is unequalled. This peculiar *tristesse* underlies his art in almost all of its manifestations. It finds voice in the finale of the "Divertimento" for violin and orchestra; it wails in the grievous tune imputed to the lamenting bagpipe-player who, in "La Cornemuse," is heard "near the crossroads of the crucifix"; it pervades his inexpressibily doleful picture of the lonely, marsh-bordered pool under ominous skies; it sings in the sweet and plaintive voice of the doomed child Tintagiles; it is sardonic, embittered, and terrible in the "Villanelle du Diable"; wild and reckless, or tragically gay, in the "Sérénade" and "Dansons la Gigue"; unutterably mournful in "Le son du Cor"; passionately rebellious in his song "Vereinsamt." This enduring melancholy is, moreover, peculiar to himself. It is a very different thing from the lucid pathos that speaks from certain songs of Schubert; from the uneasy and passionate brooding of Chopin; from the heart-shaking sorrow that fills up the third act of Wagner's "Tristan"; from the wistful self-communing of Schumann; from the black despair that tortured the soul of Tchaikovsky; from the tender and elegiacal regret which in Edward Mac-

Dowell finds a matchless declaration;
from the passive, almost inarticulate sorrow, the "dim sadness" (in Milton's
phrase), that inhabits certain wonderful
pages of Debussy's "Pelléas." It is different from these—a sadness more subtle,
more bitter, more tenacious, more deep-
seated; it is an emotional nuance that
Loeffler alone has felt and expressed.

Despite his occasional utterance of
more serene and buoyant moods, he is
evidently at heart one of "the children
of sorrow"—one of that troubled and
spiritually restless clan which has num-
bered among its members Leopardi and
Heine, Poe and Rossetti and Mangan,
Baudelaire and Verlaine, Chopin, Schumann, Tchaikovsky. The artist in whom
sensibility and emotion predominate over
aspiration comes inevitably to regard the
world as a *via dolorosa* of defeated
dreams. He sees love, "beautiful like
the autumn evening, dumb like the
autumn evening, fading like the autumn

evening." He sees beauty and desire, ardour and hope, wane with the inexorable march of the years; he sees the spreading of "the world's slow stain." So that he comes to ask himself: Whence springs that profound and inscrutable melancholy which falls upon us at the moment when we are about to consummate some long-cherished and ardently envisaged dream? Of what origin are the vague, anonymous regrets, the nameless misgivings, the mysterious hesitancies, which beset us at such a time and stale the wine of our delight? Why is it that at the very instant when we behold our dream incarnate in the warm and living present, when we are at last face to face with it in all its glowing and longed-for actuality, we find ourselves afflicted with a sudden numbness, a palsy of the soul, so that happiness has passed us by and we have not felt its touch: has cheated us while in the act of seeming to appease? Is it ordained that our desires shall never flower for us in their perfection? Is there no sustenance for the dreaming heart and the dream-filled mind but Dead Sea fruit?—It would seem that this is so, when those dreams, those desires, are woven of that fabric which is dyed in the colours of mortality: that perishable vesture with which men seek to clothe themselves in happiness or peace. It would seem that the joy which cometh in the morning is no joy at all, but sorrow and emptiness, save when we send it up to God in songs or out to other hearts in selflessness. For it is given to any of us, miraculously enough, to achieve, if only for a brief unforgettable moment, the clarified and serene and infinitely joyous vision of which Plato tells us in the Phædo, whereby we may share the felicity of those who dwell among the immortals—"who see the moon and stars as they really are, and whose happiness in other matters is of a piece with this."